SWIM BETTER, SWIM FASTER

SWIM BETTER, SWIM FASTER

PAUL MASON

B L O O M S B U R Y

LONDON · NEW DELHI · NEW YORK · SYDNEY

Note
While every effort has been made to ensure that the content of this book is as technically accurate and as sound as possible, neither the author nor the publishers can accept responsibility for any injury or loss sustained as a result of the use of this material.

Published by Bloomsbury Publishing Plc
50 Bedford Square
London WC1B 3DP
www.bloomsbury.com

First edition 2014

ISBN (print): 978-1-4081-8654-1
ISBN (ePdf): 978-1-4081-8655-8
ISBN (EPUB): 978-1-4081-8656-5

A CIP catalogue record for this book is available from the British Library.

Acknowledgements
Cover photograph © Brian Stevenson/Aurora/Getty Images
Inside photographs © Paul Mason, further photo credits listed on page 6
Illustrations by Tom Croft
Commissioned by Lisa Thomas

This book is produced using paper that is made from wood grown in managed, sustainable forests. It is natural, renewable and recyclable. The logging and manufacturing processes conform to the environmental regulations of the country of origin.

Typeset in 10pt on 13 MetalPlus by seagulls.net

Printed and bound in China by C&C Offset Printing Co

10 9 8 7 6 5 4 3 2 1

CONTENTS

Acknowledgements 6
Introduction 8

01 Swimming is simple 13
02 Flexibility 21
03 Body position 39
04 Arm stroke 57
05 Breathing 75
06 Kicking 89
07 Stroke and rhythm 103
08 Turns 117
09 Open water 129

Technique training sessions 150
About the author 157
Index 158

ACKNOWLEDGEMENTS

More than anyone this book is for my Dad, who spent years waking me at 5.30 a.m. and driving me to the pool, and never complained once. He would have been tickled pink to see some of the knowledge I gained going back out into the world of swimming.

Thanks to Emma Mason for her irreplaceable help while the photos were being taken. Big thanks to the folks at the photo locations, particularly Sao at Quinta Raposeiras, Portugal; also everyone at Arena, Biarritz, and the pool staff at One Shenton, Singapore.

All photos © Paul Mason, with the exception of those on pages: 5 © Hiper Com/Shutterstock; 7 (bottom) © Friso Gentsch/DPA; 7 (top), 12–13, 18, 2–21, 34, 37, 38–39, 55, 56–57, 64, 77 (both), 79, 87, 88–89, 101, 120, 128–129, 131 (both), 132, 146, 154–155 © Shutterstock; 11 © David Madison/Getty Images; 18–19 (across middle) © Arztsamui/ Shutterstock; 19 (right) and 55 © BrunoRosa/ Shutterstock; 74–74 © Herbert Kratky/Shutterstock. 78 © Ralf Herschbach/Shutterstock; 92 © Frank Gunn/The Canadian Press/Press Association Images; 99 © Bob Thomas/Getty Images; 102–103 and 137 © Stefan Holm/Shutterstock; 113 © Maxisport/Shutterstock; 114 © Africa Rising/ Shutterstock; 114–115 © July Store/Shutterstock; 118–119 © Michael Sohn/AP/Press Association Images; 130 © Rob Wilson/Shutterstock; 133 © Alain Lauga/Shutterstock; 134 © David Ebener/ DPA/Press Association Images; 143 © Steve Parsons/PA Archive/Press Association Images; 144 © Alberto Loyo/Shutterstock; 148–149 © sinister pictures/Demotix/Press Association Images.

INTRODUCTION

swim *verb* bathe, dip, be awash, glide, move through water using natural means of propulsion

This book grew out of the experience of coaching swimmers. Not top-level racers striving for national championships or dreaming of Olympic glory. Ordinary swimmers. The ones who fall somewhere between Becky Adlington and people who would only swim if they fell out of a boat.

In other words, most of us.

IS THIS BOOK FOR YOU?

There are lots of good books on swimming out there. To work out if this particular one will help you, ask yourself if you fit into one of these categories:

- Are you a keen swimmer who turns up at the pool and regularly swims for half an hour or more, getting fitter and fitter – but never much faster?
- Does it feel as though you're splashing your way up and down the pool, while you notice the really good swimmers smoothly gliding along?
- Would you like to be able to do triathlons, but find the swim leg so daunting that it puts you off?
- Do you find swimming front crawl so tiring that you can only manage a couple of lengths at a time – even though you can swim breaststroke for ages?
- Are you aiming to take part in a long swim for charity and feeling nervous about completing the distance, or maybe wishing you could swim front crawl instead of breaststroke?

If you read one or more of these and felt a flash of recognition, *Swim Better, Swim Faster* can help.

SIX SIMPLE ELEMENTS

Swim Better, Swim Faster separates front crawl into six key elements. Work on just one of these for even a few hours, and you should feel an improvement in your stroke:

1. Flexibility
2. Body position
3. Arm stroke
4. Breathing
5. Kicking
6. Stroke and rhythm

People often feel that they have a particular problem with one of these areas, and concentrate on that. But the trick with swimming is to get *all* the elements of your stroke working together smoothly and in balance. Work on all six over a period of time, and your swimming will quickly improve.

TURNS

As well as swimming technique, *Swim Better, Swim Faster* has advice on turns:

- Many pool swimmers would like to learn tumble turns, which are a great way of getting more out of your time in the pool.
- Triathletes taking part in cold-weather races often do the swim leg in a pool. In some triathlons swimmers are banned from doing tumble turns – but it's still possible to make up a lot of time by doing the fastest possible touch turn.

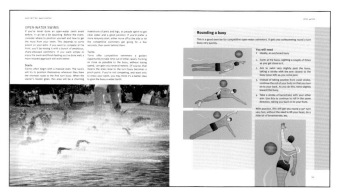

Top tip

The advice and drills in *Swim Better, Swim Faster* will make you a good freestyle swimmer. But improvement doesn't stop there.

BECOME YOUR OWN COACH

This really works: after over 40 years of swimming, I still think about my technique on just about every length I swim, try new things, and develop new ways of training.

Always be careful, though, about picking up bits and pieces of advice from the internet. There's more than one style of swimming front crawl. The technique in this book is good for swimming middle and longer distances, but may not be what a typical sprinter would use. Mixing and matching from different styles isn't likely to help your stroke.

OPEN WATER

Open-water swimming – in lakes, rivers and the sea – is a fast-growing area of the sport. The back-to-nature vibe, and the fact that it's generally free, fits the spirit of the times. But if you're used to pools, swimming in open water requires adaptations to your approach. You also need one or two extra pieces of equipment. See page 130 to find out more.

RAPID IMPROVEMENTS

Putting *Swim Better, Swim Faster* into action should lead to noticeable gains within a relatively short time. Swimmers often report a measureable improvement within three or four hours. Within 10 to 12 hours, most people find their stroke has become smoother and more efficient.

To help you get maximum benefit from the book, starting on page 151 you'll find suggested training sessions. Each session focuses on a different aspect of your front-crawl style, and is between 20 and 40 minutes long. If you have more time than this, it's easy to combine the main sets from different sessions together.

FOCUS YOUR TRAINING

Always distinguish working on your technique from training for fitness. You learn new techniques best when fresh and rested. Never nail technique work onto the end of a fitness-based session: you'll be too tired to do the work properly.

USING THE BOOK

Each of the technique sections of this book has the same structure:

- First there's an introduction to the subject and the key elements that will improve your stroke, saying what you're trying to achieve.
- There's also information on some of the common problems swimmers experience, and suggestions for ways to check which areas you need to work on.
- Finally, there are drills that will help you to improve. If there's more than one drill, the simplest and/or most basic comes first, then they get steadily more advanced.

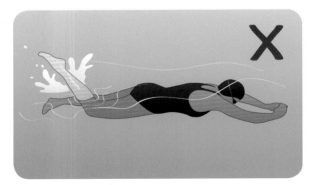

▲ A poor kicking style, with very bent knees. This will hold the swimmer back by creating drag and affecting her body position. She needs to remember the coaching maxim 'kick water not air'

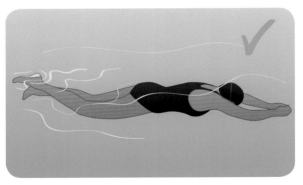

▲ This swimmer has a much neater swimming technique: most of the movement comes from her hips, not her knees, and she is kicking mostly underwater with only her heels breaking the surface.

01
SWIMMING IS SIMPLE

swim *verb* float, glide, slip, stroke, submerge, move or propel yourself through water using natural means such as arms and legs

SWIMMING IS SIMPLE

At heart, swimming is simple. The basic techniques – arm pull and recovery, kick, and body movement – aren't especially complicated. But unless you've been a competitive swimmer, you probably don't really have a clear idea of what you should be trying to achieve. This chapter gives you that information.

WHAT YOU'RE AIMING FOR

Aim for a smooth stroke, your body rolling from side to side with each arm stroke, but always straight and level in the water. Breathing should be a seamless part of the side-to-side roll that comes with each arm stroke. Your legs kick in a rhythm that matches your arms.

FRONT CRAWL ARM PULL

Each front crawl arm pull should be a smooth arm movement. However, when thinking about your technique it's useful to divide each arm stroke into four stages:

1. Entry
2. Catch
3. Pull
4. Recovery

The underwater part of each stroke begins slow and gets faster. Your hand accelerates, moving faster as you reach the end of the pull.

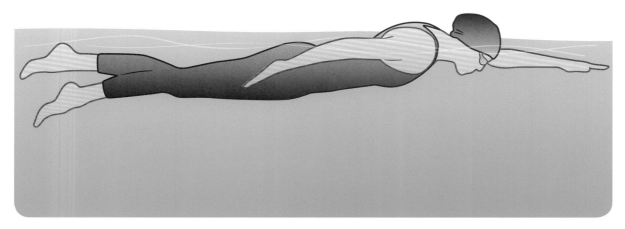

Stage 1: Entry

Your arm enters the water fingertips first, with the thumb side angled slightly downward. It goes in level with your shoulder (rather than your nose). Your hand then stretches forward, still off centre, and turns so that it's flat to the bottom of the pool.

Stage 2: Catch

Your arm begins to bend and your hand sweeps downward, with your elbow bent and staying high. At this point your body has rolled, so that the pulling side is slightly down and the other side slightly up. This stage of your stroke feels like a powered glide, maintaining your speed but not increasing it.

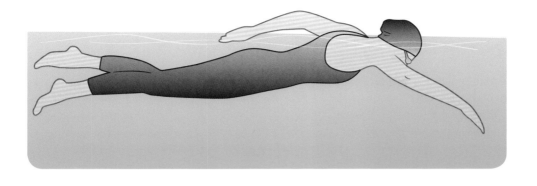

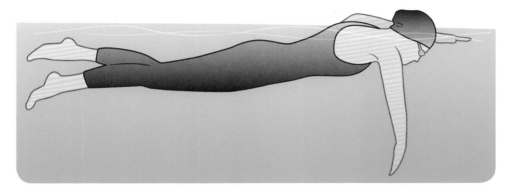

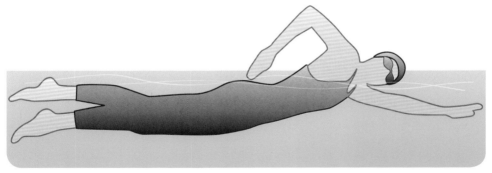

Stage 3: Pull

The pull is the stage that adds speed. Most swimmers pull in a slightly curved path. Their hand sweeps in from the line of their shoulder to just inside the outer line of their body, then out again to leave the water with their thumb brushing their hip or thigh. Other swimmers find that a feeling of pulling straight back works best (though the roll of their body means they don't actually pull straight backward).

Stage 4: Recovery

Your elbow leaves the water before your hand, and leads the recovery. Leading with your hand rather than your elbow is a common mistake. It often causes the body to twist and kink, rather than keeping in a straight line. It's important to relax your arm during the recovery, as this helps you swim smoothly.

BREATHING

Breathing is one of the things lots of untrained swimmers have trouble with. Often it's because they're turning their head to breathe by twisting their neck around, lifting their chin, or both. This makes your stroke lumpy and uneven, and tends to lead to snaking along the pool when you should be arrowing.

Good swimmers make taking a breath part of the natural roll of their body. Their face comes smoothly out of the water as their pull finishes. They take a breath in the first part of the recovery stage, and during the second part their face rotates back below the surface.

Many swimmers breathe every two strokes, always on the same side of their body. This isn't ideal, as it means their stroke and body position is biased to one side. It's much better to train yourself to breathe every three strokes.

Count your strokes

Before you start putting *Swim Better, Swim Faster* into practice, count how many strokes on average it takes you to swim a length of front crawl. This is your baseline for working out if your stroke is improving. Fewer strokes per length = a more efficient stroke.

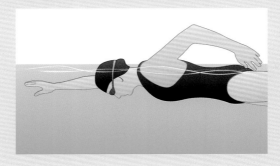

Watch other swimmers

If you see someone with a really good stroke, try to fix how it looks in your mind's eye. Imagine yourself swimming the same way. While you're swimming along, make a comparison – are my arms going at the same speed? Am I gliding in the same way? Is my body rolling from side to side like his/hers?

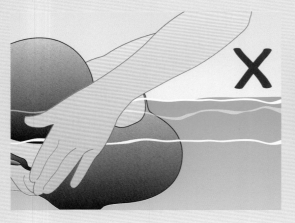

BODY POSITION

Your body should always be in a straight line pointing toward the end of the pool, like a pencil floating on the surface. One common way of expressing this is to imagine you're a human kebab, with an unbendable metal stick running from head to heels. You may prefer to imagine your body is contained in a tube: you can rotate inside it, but you mustn't touch the sides.

KICKING

Kicking for front crawl is the opposite of what Austrian ski instructors always used to shout: do *not* bend the knees. At least, not deliberately. Big knee-based kicks create so much turbulence and drag that they actually slow you down. They also wreak havoc with your body position, wagging your bottom about or causing your hips to drop. Instead aim to kick from your hips. Keep your knees stiff (but not rigid) and your ankles relaxed.

Front crawl swimmers generally use one, two or three kicks per arm stroke. Two works well for most people, but it's more important that your technique is good than that you match a particular number.

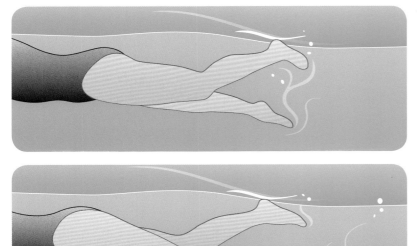

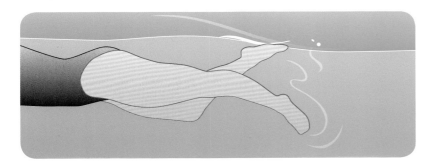

◀ Front crawl kick is done in a smooth, continuous movement. Notice how the swimmer always has one leg almost straight, while the other is only ever slightly bent. This is because she is kicking from the hips, not the knees. The swimmer's feet never break the surface: every up and down movement acts on the water, not the air. Big splashes may look fast, but in reality they usually slow you down.

EQUIPMENT

One of the nice things about swimming is that you don't have to drag loads of equipment around with you. Two things that are essential, if you don't own them already, are a proper costume and some goggles.

- A fitted costume is important because anything that drags, such as loose shorts for men, will slow you down and give a false impression of how well (or rather, how badly) you're swimming.
- Goggles allow you to see what your hands are doing underwater and whether you're swimming in a straight line.
- Earplugs are also a good idea: otherwise, the noise and sensation of having your ears fill with water, especially in drills where you're swimming on your side, can be really annoying.

Most of the drills in this book can be done without any additional kit, but there's some equipment that comes in handy if you want to invest in it:

- Swim fins – *not* diving fins. Swim fins are shorter and tend to be made of softer rubber. They should fit closely, but without being super-tight.
- Kickboard (for holding onto while swimming legs-only) and pull buoy (to put between your thighs while doing arms-only). Pools usually have these available if you ask, but it's better to bring your own. Kickboards provided by the pool are often too small, meaning you have to use two stacked up.
- Swimming snorkel, which rises in front of your face and is handy in some drills and for practising

kick. If you use one of these, you'll also need a nose clip.

- Ankle band: this is a rubber band that goes around your ankles, making sure you don't cheat when you're supposed to be swimming arms-only. You can make these out of old bike inner tubes.
- A rubber hat if you have long hair (which otherwise will drag and affect your head position).

▲ If you're taking part in a triathlon, a specialist tri-suit, which can be worn during all three legs – swim, bike and run – is useful. In cold water, triathletes swim wearing a wetsuit, which makes you more streamlined and buoyant.

Keys to success

- Count your strokes on every length to get an idea of how your stroke is working. As your stroke becomes more efficient, your should find you are taking fewer strokes per length when swimming at the same pool.

- Swim with a smooth arm and leg action, moving continuously; avoid jerky, splashy actions

- Keep your body straight. Side-to-side roll is good, but twisting and kinking is bad

02

FLEXIBILITY

flexible *adj.* lissom, supple, lithe, elastic, able to bend or be bent repeatedly without damage or injury

FLEXIBILITY

This chapter comes *before* the technique sections for a reason. Put simply, if you lack flexibility, there are some elements of swimming technique you'll never be able to manage. People with stiff neck, shoulders and back find it particularly hard to master technique, but overall flexibility is important in swimming.

STRETCHING TECHNIQUES

Never do any stretch to a point where it hurts. You need to be able to feel a bit of pull in the muscles

Use your breath

When you've taken a stretch as far as is comfortable, concentrate on breathing deeply, from your stomach rather than your chest. It helps you relax and get a little more from the stretch.

you're stretching, but if it starts to hurt, gently ease out of the stretch and try again. It's best to time your movement into the stretch to happen as you breathe

22

out. If you need to take a breath, stop moving while you breathe in.

INCREASING FLEXIBILITY

To improve their swimming, most people also need to improve their general flexibility. A great way to do this is to take a yoga course. There are lots of different schools of yoga: a gentle one may be best. Scaravelli yoga seems to be useful for swimming, but it's not that common, and it can be hard to find courses. Hatha yoga is a good alternative.

The exercises on the following pages are mainly targeted at swimming (apart from pages 24–27). You can do them just about anywhere: sitting in front of the TV, on the poolside, out in the garden. Try to do some flexibility work every day – 15 minutes spent on this pays dividends in the pool.

WARMING UP AND WARMING DOWN

As well as using stretches to improve your flexibility, make them part of every swimming session. Spend 10 minutes at the start and finish of every session doing some stretching. At the start, it prepares your muscles for what's coming; at the finish, it will reduce any muscle soreness and fatigue you feel the next day. Dynamic stretches are best for warming up, static ones for warming down.

23

GENERAL FLEXIBILITY

As a simple, time-effective way of improving your general flexibility, it's hard to beat a bit of yoga. In particular, try following the lead of millions of people and starting each day with a sun salute or two. It's helpful to have a yoga mat for this, but I do it most mornings on an old carpet and have yet to suffer any ill effects.

Sun salute

There are slightly differing versions of the sun salute: what's shown here seems to work well for swimming and cycling.

1. Stand in balance, heels on the floor, feet shoulder-width apart. Be careful not to stick your bottom out. Reach your arms above your head and extend them, but without altering your body position.
2. Bend forward from the waist, keeping your arms stretched out and your feet flat. Touch the ground with your hands, or get as close as you can to that. Relax your jaw, neck, back and stomach so that you're dangling from the waist. Breathe deeply.

Steps 1 and 2 alone are an excellent stretch to do as a way of relaxing your jaw, neck and back muscles.

1

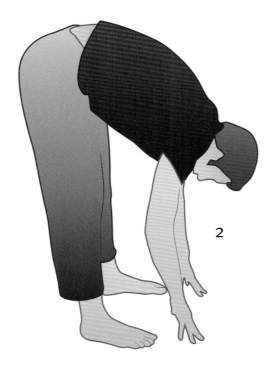

2

3. Place your hands on the floor. Bend one leg, and place the other one straight back behind you. Drop your hips (make sure not to twist them sideways), and feel the stretch in your groin.

4. Bring the bent leg back beside the extended one, so that you end up in a dead-straight press-up position. Hold this – it can be a bit of a trembler – for two or three breaths.

Hold each pose

Spend a little time in each pose. Holding each one for about five deep, long breaths is usually about right.

5. Drop your knees to the floor and, keeping your arms stretched out in front of you, scrunch up like someone praying.

6. Pivot forward and drop your hips to the floor, arching your lower back while extending through the shoulders and neck and pushing up with straight arms. Imagine your head is lifting upward, and avoid arcing your neck back.

7. Push up on to all fours, with straight back legs and bent at the waist. You're aiming to make an upside-down V shape. Keep your legs and arms as straight as possible, and if you can manage it have your feet flat on the floor (this isn't crucial). Relax, especially your shoulders, neck and jaw. It should feel as if your head is dangling loosely between your shoulders.

8. Step forward with the same leg as stepped back in step 3 of the sun salute. You should find yourself in a mirror image of the position from step 3.

9. Return to the position shown in step 2 of the sun salute.

10. Either finish as in step 1, but in reverse: standing back up with straight arms out in front and your weight on the balls of your feet. Or, ending with your arms hanging down at your sides. In this, try to imagine each individual vertebra straightening, starting from the very bottom of your spine. Let your arms dangle loosely, and keep your neck and jaw relaxed.

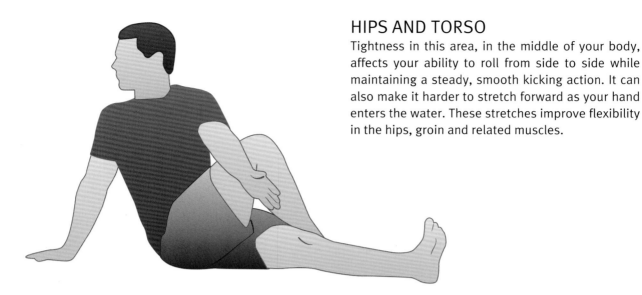

HIPS AND TORSO

Tightness in this area, in the middle of your body, affects your ability to roll from side to side while maintaining a steady, smooth kicking action. It can also make it harder to stretch forward as your hand enters the water. These stretches improve flexibility in the hips, groin and related muscles.

Hip stretch 1

Sit down with your legs out straight in front of you. Bent and lift your right leg, placing your foot on the outside of your left knee. Turn to the right, keeping your hips level and your bottom flat on the ground. Place your left forearm outside your right knee then gently move your right knee outward. Hold for five deep breaths, then repeat on the other side.

Hip stretch 2

From a standing position, take a lunge step forward. Kneel on your rear knee: this knee needs to be behind your hip. Cup your hands over your front knee, then move your hips forward until you feel the stretch in your hip and upper thigh. Your front knee should be at an angle of at least 90°. Hold the stretch for several deep, long breaths, then repeat with the other leg.

Side stretch

This simple stretch is great is you're having trouble extending forward after your hand enters the water. Concentrate on breathing deeply and relaxing into the stretch.

Stand in the starting position for the sun salute (see page 24). Make sure your hips are tucked in and relaxed, and your feet shoulder-width apart (this is closer together than most people think – use a mirror or the reflection in a window to check, if you can). Bring your arms above your head, and hold your left wrist with your right hand.

Lean to the right: take care to keep your body facing forward, don't let yourself turn your shoulders or hips in the direction of the stretch. When you feel a stretch down your side, hold the position for several deep breaths, then return to the starting point. Repeat for the other side.

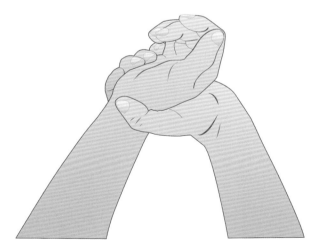

SHOULDERS AND NECK

These two stretches help with your shoulder mobility, which is crucial for swimming front crawl. Doing them regularly makes stretching forward after your arm has entered the water much easier. This starts your body rolling and puts it in the correct position for the rest of the arm pull.

Don't worry if you find these stretches easier on one side than the other – almost everyone has the same experience.

Crossed-forearms stretch

1. Stand or sit upright looking straight ahead, with your shoulders relaxed. Take a deep breath, and as you let it out, bring your arms up and forward, and cross them at the elbows.
2. Bring the forearm of the lower arm inward, and cup your fingertips in the heel of the other hand. Take another deep breath and relax your jaw and shoulders, letting the shoulders drop. Try to keep them in this position throughout.
3. Slowly lift your elbows up and forward (don't forget to keep your shoulders relaxed). As your elbows rise, you should feel the stretch engage different muscles between your shoulder blades. Move your elbows up and down slowly several times, holding them in position and taking a couple of deep breaths if you feel an area of tightness.
4. Release, and repeat with the opposite elbow highest.

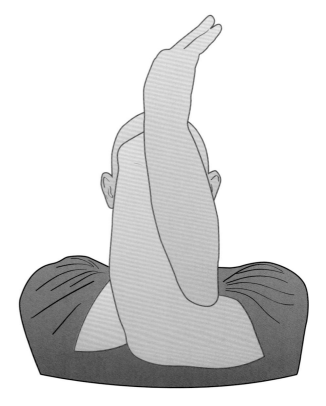

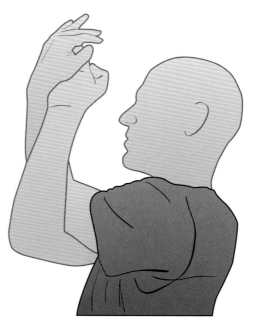

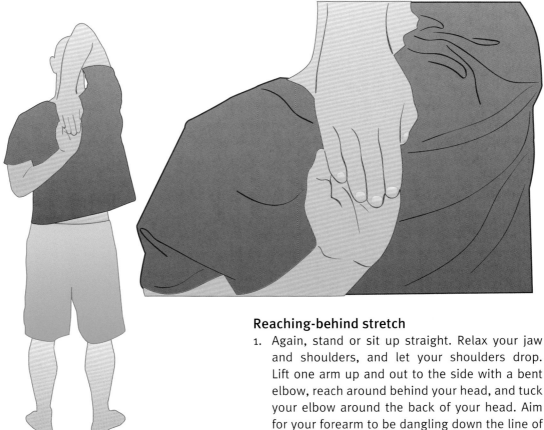

Reaching-behind stretch

1. Again, stand or sit up straight. Relax your jaw and shoulders, and let your shoulders drop. Lift one arm up and out to the side with a bent elbow, reach around behind your head, and tuck your elbow around the back of your head. Aim for your forearm to be dangling down the line of your spine.

2. Bring your other arm behind your back, letting the back of your hand rest at the base of your spine. Bend your elbow, and work your hand up the line of your spine. You're aiming for the back of your hand to be resting between your shoulder blades.

3. Try to place the palms of your hands together. Don't overstrain this stretch: as ever, this is likely to cause injury. Very few people can manage this stretch first go (even second, or twenty-second go). You may only be able to get your fingertips to touch, or not be able to touch your hands at all. Don't worry, this is a *good* thing – it means you have an obvious area where your swimming stroke can be improved.

Never clench!

Some people learn a version of this stretch in which they link their fingers together, like one Action Man stopping another from plunging into a chasm. This can lead to overstretching or injury; it's best just to let your hands touch.

LEGS

It's not immediately apparent, but relaxed, flexible legs are important when swimming freestyle. Your kicking action should be light and loose, coming from the hips: anything else is likely to upset your stroke. You'll only achieve this 'flutter kick' if your legs and ankles are flexible.

Leg stretch 1

Stand well away from a wall, with your feet shoulder-width apart. Lean forward and rest your palms against the wall, stepping one leg forward too. The other leg stays straight, with your foot flat on the floor and pointing forward. Bend your elbows and feel the stretch in the back of your leg.

After several deep, slow breaths, return to the starting position and repeat the exercise with the other leg stretched out behind. Finally, place both feet together and repeat once more.

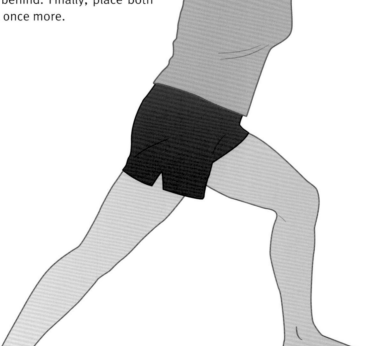

Leg stretch 2

This one is good for your hamstrings if you've ridden a bike to the pool. Sit up straight, with your legs out in front of you and your toes pointing up in the air. Move one foot back, sliding the sole along the calf and thigh of your other leg.

Staying upright, reach forward with both hands and place your fingertips on the toes of the foot pointing up in the air. Hold the stretch for five deep breaths or so, return to the starting position, and repeat for the other leg.

Leg stretch 3

Stand upright, next to a wall if your balance isn't great. Lift one foot behind you, hold it with your hand, and press your heel into your bottom. Here you might need to grab something for balance. Hold the stretch while you breathe deeply several times, release your foot and let it swing gently forward. Repeat using the other leg.

Take care with this stretch not to arch your lower back when you pull your foot in: your hips should stay level with the ground.

WARMING UP

Stretching has a part to play in warming up before a training session (whether it's a technique session or a fitness one). Lots of English people feel embarrassed about stretching on the side of the pool – it's seen as a bit effete or unnecessary. But warming up properly prepares your body for exercise, making injury much less likely.

Warming up – legs

If you can, one of the best ways of getting your body systems going before a swimming session is to cycle to the pool. A distance of about 10km will wake your muscles up to the fact that they're exercising, prepare the joints in your hips, knees and ankles, and lift your heart rate. Don't race: just go at a speed that would make holding a conversation moderately tricky.

◄ Most people have one area of
▼ their body that needs a little extra flexibility work. If you're a keen cyclist it may be your hamstrings. If you sit at a desk all day, that can result in tight hip flexor muscles. If you do have an area of particular inflexibility, it's worth getting expert advice about how to address it, because the problem doesn't always originate from the place where you can feel the stiffness.

Once you get to the pool, you'll need to stretch your hamstrings a bit, because cycling only offers them a limited range of movement. The stretch at the top of page 33 is good for this.

Warming up – shoulders and upper body

Your shoulders will need a bit more work, because they haven't been doing much on the bike. Start with the stretches on pages 30 and 31, and the forward bend from page 24 (this does have a slightly 1930s-Swedish-exercise feel to it, but is very effective nonetheless).

Warm up your shoulders further with some active movement. Do this one arm at a time. Windmill your arm backward, a bit like doing backstroke. Start slowly, trying to relax your shoulder so that there's no creaking, clicking or straining. Steadily build up the speed of the windmills until you feel a slight tingling in your fingertips. Maintain the movement for 10 full windmills, and stop. Breathe out and relax your shoulders, then repeat with the other arm.

Next do the whole thing again, but this time with each arm windmilling forward, a bit like doing freestyle.

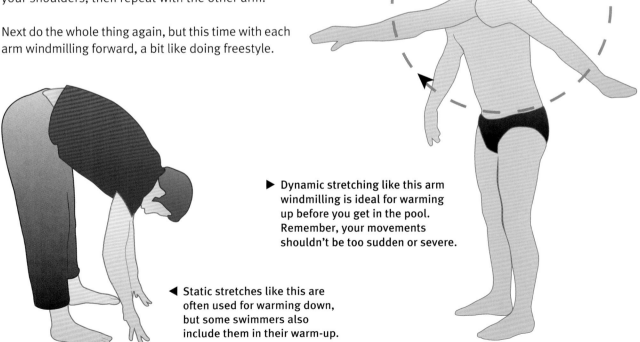

▶ Dynamic stretching like this arm windmilling is ideal for warming up before you get in the pool. Remember, your movements shouldn't be too sudden or severe.

◀ Static stretches like this are often used for warming down, but some swimmers also include them in their warm-up.

WARMING DOWN

Including a proper warm-down in your swimming routine has several benefits. The key one is that a warm-down containing some stretching will prevent or ease the muscle soreness you feel later.

For swimmers, a warm-down in two parts is a good idea:

1. Swim a reasonable distance (for most people, between 100m and 400m is about right) at a steady pace. Don't crawl along so slowly you're practically sinking, just don't push things. Concentrate on keeping your stroke long and balanced, trying to glide through the water.

2. Do a few key stretches. My favourites are the shoulder stretches from pages 30 and 31, the forward bend from page 24, and the leg stretch from page 32. You'll find the ones that work for you: the areas where you tend to feel muscle soreness will guide you, but don't forget that this will change as your stroke develops.

EATING

Try to eat something – a banana, a sandwich or a flapjack, something that has a carbohydrate element – within 15 minutes or so of finishing a training session. This is a window of time in which your body efficiently replaces the muscle energy that is burned during demanding exercise.

In general, swimming doesn't require a special diet. Just try to eat a balance of different foods, and avoid too many fatty, fried meals and alcohol. If you're swimming partly with the aim of losing weight, bear in mind that the only way to do this is to burn more calories than you eat, which will cause feelings of hunger.

Keys to success

- It's OK to concentrate a bit more on specific areas, but make sure your flexibility training encompasses your whole body

- Try to work flexibility exercises into your daily routine: always do them when a particular TV programme starts or finishes, or before breakfast, for example

- Always include stretching in your swimming sessions, both at the start and the finish

03
BODY POSITION

position *noun* place, arrangement, posture, location, situation, setting, the posture that somebody's body is in, the way or direction in which an object is placed or arranged

BODY POSITION

WHAT YOU'RE AIMING FOR

The aim in swimming is always to find a more streamlined position. This allows you to glide along, rather than fighting your way down the pool. There are four key elements to a good streamlined style:

1. The right head angle
2. Correct chest and hip position
3. Good body roll
4. Eliminating twist

HEAD ANGLE

The angle at which you hold your head has a big effect, because it's linked to your upper body. This in turn affects your hips, which in turn affect your leg kick. Most swimmers hold their heads too high (partly as a result of the need to see where you're going in a public pool).

Aim to swim looking at the bottom of the pool, perhaps very slightly ahead but with your neck basically in line with your body. You can experiment with head position while swimming along: too low will immediately be obvious, you'll be able to feel it slowing you down. Too high and it will drag your hips down, and you'll feel like a lifeguard crashing out through the surf.

The correct angle is a happy medium of possible head positions. Much higher or lower and it will cause drag.

▲ The top photo shows
◄ a swimmer with his head too high, which will cause his hips to sink. In the middle image his head has drifted too low: even his shoulder is catching water and creating drag. In the final image, the swimmer's head position is ideal.

Top tip

Try to make sure your head stays as still as possible while you swim. One tip that will help you do this is:

KEEP THE TOP OF YOUR HEAD IN ONE SPOT

As you swim along, look down at the bottom of the pool. Imagine that the top of your head has a dot on top of it, pointing straight at the end of the lane.

To someone watching, the dot shouldn't move much, or at all. Even as your head turns for a breath, the dot stays steady.

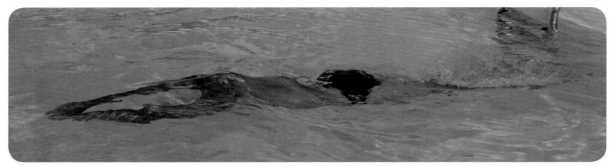

▲ Pushing off the wall in a streamlined position

▲ Practising a streamlined kick using a swimming snorkel

SHOULDER AND HIP POSITION

When swimming, aim for your shoulders and hips to be at roughly the same level in the water, just below the surface. Most people naturally hold their body a little bit bent forward, so to be dead flat you have to slightly extend your chest, stomach and hips, as in the drill on page 43.

Hip dragger or bottom waggler?

Swimmers with their chest and hips in an inefficient, draggy position are a common sight in pools around the world. The two key problems are dragging your hips (swimming with them lower in the water than your chest), and lifting your hips so that your bottom sticks up. It's hard to know for yourself if you have either of these problems, so ask a friend to watch you swim and tell you.

Hip draggers: Hip dragging is often caused by a poor catch (see page 64), a weak or poor leg kick (for advice on how to improve this, see pages 92–109) or a too-high head position (see pages 40–41). It's often also linked to a lack of flexibility in your hips: see page 28 for exercises that can help improve this.

Bottom wagglers: Bottom waggling often happens when swimmers have a poor kicking technique or a too-low head position. Using the head position on page 40 may get rid of the problem. It's also useful to work on improving extension through the chest and stomach, pushing down slightly with the buttocks and opening the hips. This should bring your head and shoulders forward and up, and your bottom down.

The streamlined position

This dry-land exercise helps you to fix muscle memory of what a streamlined body position feels like.

What you need
- A wall at least 2.5m high, in a warm room

Stand with your back against the wall. In order, place your heels, bottom, shoulder blades and the back of your head against the wall. Step forward, trying to keep this straight-line shape. Step back, and see if you've succeeded. At first, most people don't – but keep trying!

Next, bring your arms up straight over your head, thumbs linked together. Press the backs of your hands against the wall, without any of the other contact points losing touch. This is a streamlined position.

See for yourself: Drag and head position

Swim a length with your usual style, counting how many strokes it takes. Rest for a minute, then swim a second length with your chin tucked into your chest, again counting strokes. After another minute, swim a third length with your chin up at the water's surface. You'll soon see how an extreme head position increases drag.

STREAMLINING

The drills on the next two pages will help you to develop a streamlined body position, with your head, shoulders, chest and hips all in the right alignment. They seem tough at first, and it might feel like you're going backward. The benefits *will* become clear when you switch to full stroke.

Top tip

If your body position needs improvement, it can sometimes be helpful to

IMAGINE YOUR CHEST (*NOT* YOUR HEAD) PRESSING DOWN INTO THE WATER

This has the effect of extending your stomach muscles and lifting your hips. It doesn't usually work on its own, but this can be a helpful tool when adapting your stroke.

Body position float

This drill appears ridiculously simple – until you try to do it. It takes some people weeks before they can manage it, but don't give up: this is a really good test of whether you can get your body into a streamlined position.

What you need

- It's not essential, but a swimming snorkel might help at first

1. Take a deep breath, and let yourself float face down in the water. Your whole body should be relaxed. You'll soon work out why some coaches call this the 'dead swimmer float': it might be a good idea to warn the lifeguards what you're up to.

2. Lift and reach your arms into the streamlined position from page 43.

3. Point your toes, and steadily bring your legs up to the surface. You're aiming to get four points of your body at the surface:

- back of your head
- back of your shoulders
- bottom
- heels

Don't force any of the movements toward the final position by kicking or using your hands: just let your body float up. Keep your neck relaxed, and look down at the bottom of the pool, rather than ahead or behind.

Streamlining

This is another very simple drill; to get benefit from it, you need to listen hard to your own body. This always applies in swimming, of course – try to feel how the water presses against your skin, where there's more resistance and where least. Water resistance is your enemy: any way you can find to avoid it will improve your swimming.

What you need
- Swim fins
- A swimming snorkel

1. Put on your fins, and push off into the streamlined position. Lay one hand on top of the other, and look at the bottom of the pool rather than looking ahead. Many swimmers find that the most streamlined head position looks down more than they expected.

2. Kick with a steady rhythm, fast enough to feel the water resistance as you move ahead. Make sure you're always kicking water, with no more than your heels breaking the surface.

3. Experiment with different head, shoulder, hip and foot positions to see how they affect water resistance. Try pressing down with your chest, extending through the stomach, tightening up your back and bottom – but always come back to the streamlined position from pages 43 and 45.

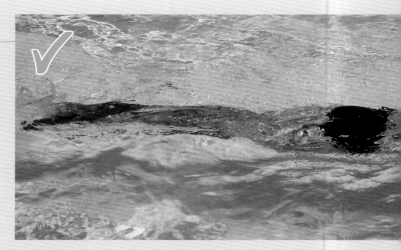

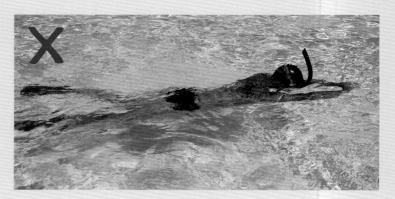

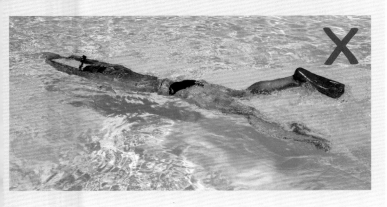

Top tip

COUNT YOUR STROKES

Counting your strokes is a good guide to how efficient your technique is becoming. As your swimming gets smoother and more streamlined, it will take fewer strokes for you to complete a length at a given speed. (Usually your stroke count rises slightly as you swim faster.) This is a rough guide to what stroke counts by an adult swimmer in a 25m pool might indicate:

25+ strokes per length: Taking this many strokes would generally mean there's plenty of room for improvement in your technique and streamlining.

20–24 strokes per length: Although at the lower end of this scale your stroke is getting pretty efficient, there are likely still to be things you can do to improve your technique.

19 strokes or fewer: This is the sort of stroke count that will look lazy to other people, but can still move you pretty quickly down the pool.

These are not rigid guidelines: some swimmers (even Olympic champions) have a high stroke count per length, while some poor swimmers have a low one. If you naturally swim with a high stroke count, don't punish yourself trying to lower it to 15. It will still be worth counting strokes, though, as the logic applies: developing a more efficient stroke will lead to a lower count.

BODY ROLL

Freestyle is sometimes called front crawl – a misleading name, as you shouldn't be spending very much time actually *on* your front. It should really be called side crawl, because most of your time is spent with your body rolled to one side or the other.

Be careful not to confuse body roll (good) with twist (so bad it should be sent to bed without any supper). Your body should keep a straight-line shape as much as possible, but your torso spins around the imaginary straight line running from your head to your feet.

There are three big advantages to rolling your body with each stroke. First, you're more streamlined and slip through the water using less energy. Second, the roll helps your leading hand extend further forward at the front of your stroke, adding to your pull. Third, it makes a smooth breathing action easier to achieve.

▼ Swimmer rolled to the side, breathing.

▲ Swimmer rolled to the same side, not breathing. Notice how the amount of body roll is similar in both photos

See for yourself: Body roll and reach

It's easy to show how rolling your body extends the reach of your stroke:

- Stand square to a table, about a metre away, and bend forward so that your torso's parallel to the ground
- Reach toward the table with one arm, as you would at the front of your freestyle stroke, but keeping your shoulders square

- Now turn your shoulders, so that the one reaching out drops and the other one rises

See how much dropping your shoulder adds to your reach?

These drills will help you develop good body roll as part of your stroke. In the second drill, the body roll is linked to taking a breath. This helps develop good, smooth breathing technique. Don't forget, though – you roll with *every* stroke, not only the ones when you take a breath.

Body roll drill 1

This drill allows you to get a feel for swimming in a streamlined position on your side.

What you need
- Pool with a line along the bottom (always try to swim straight along the line)
- Swim fins

1. Push off, and take one arm pull with your right arm. After taking the pull, lay your right arm along your side.

2. Stretch your left arm out in front, dropping your shoulder (as in the exercise on page 49).

Your head will turn to the side – just let it turn with your body, don't twist your neck – and your right shoulder, arm and hip will lift out of the water, so you're swimming along on your side.

3. Swim like this for a steady count of four, turn your head to take a breath, and carry on. Swim a whole length like this, with your right side up; repeat with your left side up on the next length.

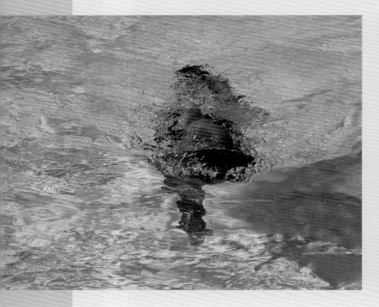

Body roll drill 2

This is a development of drill 1, but it adds a change of sides. Don't worry overmuch if your breathing needs work (just turn to Chapter 5 for advice) – in this drill, the focus is on getting used to swimming in a streamlined position on both sides.

What you need
- Pool with a straight line along the bottom
- Swim fins

1. Push off along the line and take one stroke with your right arm, as in the drill on the previous page.

2. Kick your legs 10 times, then take a stroke with your left arm while recovering your right arm. As you do this, your body rolls to the other side and you can take a breath.

3. Repeat this drill all the way down the length of the pool.

Top tip

As a way of controlling your head angle,

USE YOUR VISION

Swim looking down at the bottom of the pool. Then, as you turn your head to breathe, aim to have your vision across the line of the water's surface. You should see the world on its side: if it looks like normal, you have tilted your head up to breathe (like the swimmer above) and compromised your streamlined position.

THE ENERGY-SAPPING EVILS OF TWIST

'Twist' is when your spine bends from side to side as you swim. Twist in your swimming stroke slows you down. It increases drag, and forces you to use more energy than necessary to move forward.

ONE SIDE OR BOTH?

Ask a friend to watch you swim, from head-on and from behind. They can tell you if your stroke has twist in it, and whether the twist is to one side or both sides.

Twist to one side

If the twist is only on one side, it is often linked to the swimmer's breathing technique. They are usually breathing only to one side of their body, which makes it harder to swim with a balanced stroke. The advice

See for yourself: twist

It's easy to demonstrate to yourself how twist affects your stroke:

- Push off the side of the pool keeping your body as straight as you can, and see how far you glide
- Push off again, but with your head and feet twisting as far to the same side as possible

You'll soon get the measure of how badly twist can slow you down

▼ This swimmer's stroke has twist on both sides of her body.

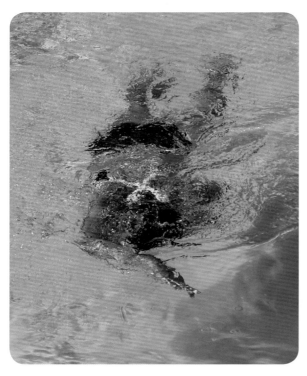

in this section will help solve the problem, but if your stroke only twists one way, it would also be a good idea to start breathing bilaterally. Pages 78–79 have more information on this.

Twist to both sides

Twist to both sides has two common causes: trying too hard, and lack of flexibility.

Swimmers trying to swim as fast as possible often throw their arms violently forward. This pulls their shoulders round, and causes their hips and legs to crab around in the same direction.

Lack of shoulder flexibility can also cause (or make worse) the twist in your stroke. Rather than extending the shoulders to reach forward and begin the arm pull, swimmers lacking shoulder flexibility have to twist their body. Because of this, the advice on the next pages should always be combined with the flexibility exercises on pages 30 and 31.

ELIMINATING TWIST

As part of your effort to eliminate twist from your stroke, try to imagine your spine is part of an inflexible steel rod running down your body from head to toe. The rod can roll, but it can't be bent.

If you don't like this image (and I don't blame you), try imagining you're swimming with your body inside a tube and it mustn't touch the sides.

Twist experiment

What you need
- Swimming pool with lines along the bottom
- Swim fins
- Mono snorkel

Find yourself a lane position that allows you to swim along above a line on the bottom of the pool. Use the line as a guide, which your head is travelling along. Concentrate on keeping your head smack in the middle of the line.

As you start each arm pull, examine how your body is affected by where you place each hand into the water. Reaching across the centre line of your body causes twist. Reaching out to the side, away from the line of your shoulders, also causes twist. You should find that the ideal entry point is somewhere more or less in line with your shoulder.

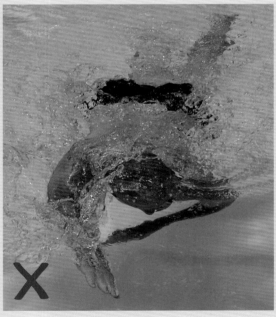

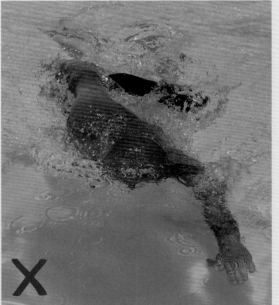

Keys to success

- Learn a flat, streamlined position, with the back of your head, shoulders, bottom and heels all just breaking the surface

- Remember: roll is good, twist is bad

- Imagine you're swimming with your body inside a tube, and you mustn't touch the sides

- Aim to breathe bilaterally (on both sides), if you don't already

04
ARM STROKE

stroke *verb* soothe, smooth, caress

noun in swimming, a single complete movement of the arms and/or legs

ARM STROKE

A lot of swimmers barely think about their arm stroke. Others look into the subject and quickly find themselves confused by the variety of advice on offer: should your hand pull in an S-shape, under your body or not, what kind of recovery should you use, and so on. In this section, you'll learn a style of arm stroke that strikes a good balance between power and streamlining.

WHAT YOU'RE AIMING FOR

Pages 14 and 15 describe the basics of a good freestyle pulling action. Overall, the key elements of the freestyle arm stroke are:

- Hand entry into the water
- The path your hand takes through the water, which can be divided into three phases: catch, in-sweep and out-sweep
- Hand shape while pulling
- Exit from the water and recovery

REDUCE DRAG, SWIM BETTER

In swimming, drag is your number one enemy. Reducing drag trumps anything else you can do to improve your technique. In your arm stroke, you can reduce drag by using a high-elbow pull. Using this, your hand enters the water in front of your shoulder. Then the path traced through the water by your hand stays outside the edge of your body for much of its time underwater.

Many swimmers use a different pull, in which they put their hand into the water right on the centre line of their body, and pull in a shape that curves in under their torso. This is more powerful than the high-elbow pull, but it creates a lot of drag. The

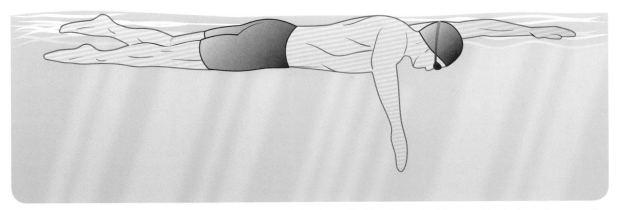

▲ Side-on view of swimmer with high-elbow action; this is also called 'early vertical forearm' technique, because the elbow is close to the surface and the forearm is pointing straight down

high-elbow pull is more streamlined, smoother, uses less energy, and makes it easier to swim at a sustained speed. This makes it especially useful for distance swims, open water and triathlon.

HAND ENTRY

Each freestyle arm stroke begins when your hand enters the water. For a high-elbow stroke, your hand needs to go in roughly in line with your shoulder. Try to slide your hand below the surface without making a big splash, by angling it slightly thumb-down. There's no need to worry too much about this, but a big, splashy hand entry means you're wasting energy by hitting against the water.

Once your hand has slid into the water, your shoulder extends and moves down, starting your body's roll to the side and allowing you to reach further ahead. At this point your hand should still be in line with your shoulder, and the back of your hand should be just below the surface.

▼ Angled hand entry

▲ Extended arm with flat hand

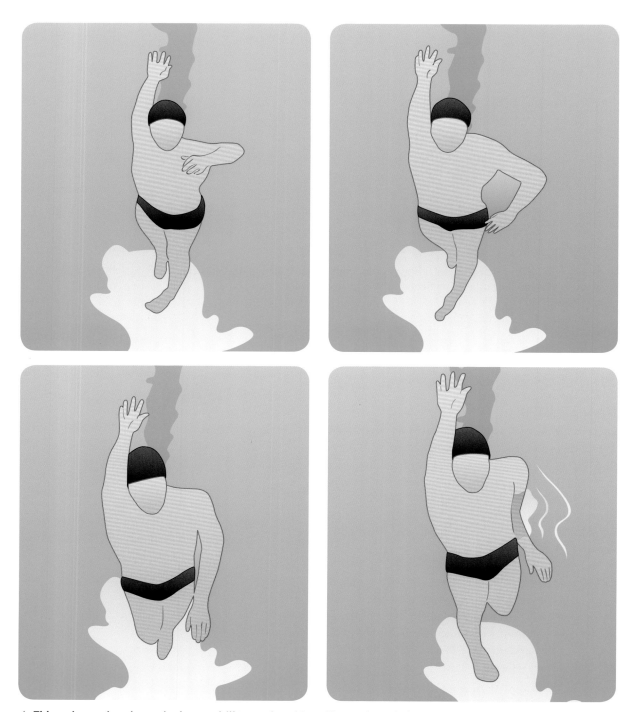

▲ This swimmer is using a single-arm drill to work on his pulling action. Find out more on pages 72–73.

UNDERWATER ACTION

Your underwater action should be one smooth movement, with your hand accelerating toward the end of the pull. It's useful, though, to separate the underwater action into three phases:

- Catch, in which your arm moves into a position in which it can start to add significant propulsion.
- In-sweep, in which your elbow is held high, bent at 90°, and your hand sweeps in toward the edge of your body
- Out-sweep, when having swept inward your hand comes out again, and leaves the water with your thumb close to or brushing your thigh.

Some swimmers prefer to simplify the arm-pull action and pull straight back using a high-elbow position rather than separating the second part of the stroke into an in-sweep and out-sweep. (The roll of their body means they are not actually likely to be pulling back in a straight line.) If you find the arm pull action tricky, this straight-back pulling action may be a better option. Be aware, though, that you do need a good streamlined position and roll in your stroke for this to work well.

THE CATCH

The catch is important because getting it right sets up the rest of your stroke. It is the transition into the most powerful part of the arm stroke, which actually drives you forward. The crucial thing to remember is that you should keep your elbow high, using it as a pivot to swing your hand down and back.

To most people, the high-elbow position feels a bit unnatural at first. Because of this, it's worth taking a bit of time to rebuild your arm stroke from the ground up. The drills shown on the next two pages are the starting point, and allow you to get a feel for the water using a high-elbow position.

▲ The catch phase for the left arm

▲ In-sweep phase: this also shows the right hand going in at an angle

▲ End of the out-sweep phase. Notice how the swimmer's arm has only ever come slightly inside the outer line of his body.

Straight-arms scull

This is a basic swimming drill that gives you a good feel for how sideways movements of your hands can provide lift and forward motion. It also introduces the slightly unnatural feeling of swimming with your arms outside the line of your body.

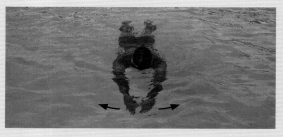

What you need
- A fairly empty pool, as you'll be moving slowly
- A swimming snorkel if you have one, so that you don't have to breathe

1. Push off the wall, and float on the surface in a streamlined position. Kick your legs in a flutter kick or use a pull buoy: the function of this is to keep your body position flat in the water, rather than to drive you forward. Have your arms relaxed and stretched out in front of you.

2. Keeping your arms straight, scull them out and in together (i.e. both arms at the same time). Have your hands angled a little downward, and scoop them around so that they're facing slightly out as you scull out, and slightly inward as you scull in.

3. Keep this motion going in a continuous rhythm, sculling your way down the lane. Experiment with different angles for your hands, to see how it affects the amount of lift and drive. Always, though, keep your arms straight and extended out in front.

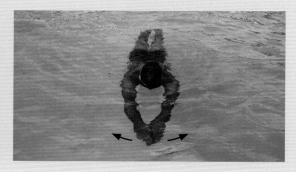

Bent-arms scull

This is a development of the drill on page 62, and starts to introduce the high-elbow position.

What you need

- A fairly empty pool, as you'll be moving slowly
- A swimming snorkel if you have one, so that you don't have to breathe

1. Push off the wall with your arms extended, as at the start of the drill on the opposite page. Kick enough to keep yourself flat in the water.

2. Instead of keeping your arms straight, bend them at the elbow. The key to this drill is that you must keep your elbows high, only just below the surface of the water.

3. Allow your hands to scull in and out, swinging below your elbows like a pair of upside-down windscreen wipers. Again, experiment with hand angles to find the greatest degree of lift and propulsion. When you can no longer see your hands in the clear part of your goggles, it's time to bring them back in again.

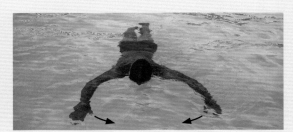

THE CATCH: HIGH-ELBOW INITIATION

Once you've done them a few times, the drills on pages 62 and 63 will give you a good feel for swimming with your arms further away from your body than most people are used to. The next two drills will help you introduce the high-elbow technique into the catch phase of your stroke.

Lane line initiation

In this drill, your elbow is kept high because it's hooked over a lane rope. This gives you a feel for initiating the catch phase with a high-elbow position.

What you need

- A tight, supportive lane rope

1. Holding on to the lane rope, place yourself at an angle of 90° to it. Float with your body at the surface in a streamlined position, kicking gently toward the rope to keep your hips and legs up. Have your arms extended in front of you.

2. Move forward so that one arm is over the rope, with the rope resting just behind the elbow. You need to be as close as possible to the position you'd take when starting an arm stroke.

3. With your head down as it would be when you're swimming, pull down and back with the arm that's hooked over the rope.

High-elbow scull

Try this drill after the exercise on page 64, and focus on keeping your elbows high.

1. Push off in a streamlined position, as you would to swim freestyle. Allow your hands to drift shoulder-width apart, so that each is in the starting position for a stroke.

2. Keeping your elbows high, use a circular sculling motion with your hand and forearm. Each hand moves slightly out, back in and toward your chest, and then forward to return to its starting point.

3. Experiment with hand angles to maximise propulsion and minimise drag where needed.

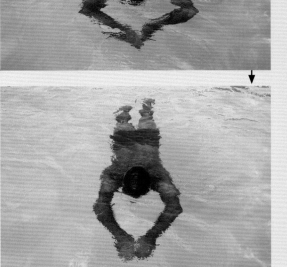

THE IN-SWEEP

The in-sweep is the phase of your stroke that follows the catch. During the in-sweep your hand sweeps back and in, toward your hips. This is where you start to generate real propulsion.

THE OUT-SWEEP

The out-sweep happens roughly halfway through your arm pull. Your hand and forearm begin to move outward, heading for the outer edge of your hip. At this point your hand is accelerating, getting faster as your elbow lifts in preparation for the hand leaving the water and the recovery phase starting.

Fixing position using edge of pool

This exercise helps you build a mental picture and muscle memory of the position of your arms at the start of the in-sweep phase.

What you need

- A pool with a raised deck (ideally with the deck about 30 cm above the surface)

1. Hold on to the side of the deck with your hands, and allow your body to sink down parallel with the wall of the pool.

2. Place your forearms flat on the deck, shoulder width apart or slightly wider and at 90° to the edge of the pool.

3. Let your body sink right down so that your weight is on your forearms and your shoulders are extended. Look straight ahead, with your head at the same angle as it would be while swimming.

▲ Correct, loose hand

HAND SHAPE

One common question from untrained swimmers is what shape they should make with their hands. Many people have been taught to swim with their hands tightly cupped, in the shape you'd use if you were trying to carry a handful of rice. In fact, you need to relax your hands and let your fingers drift slightly apart, while keeping them in a natural, curved-forward position. This sets up turbulence between your fingers and improves your hold on the water.

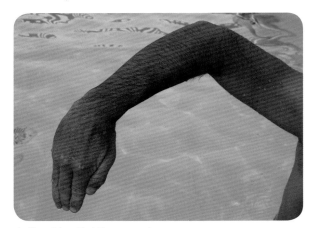

▲ Hand too tightly cupped

▲ Fingers too far apart

See for yourself

To find out for yourself the best hand shape for getting a good hold on the water, go back to the sculling drill on page 63. Try it with your fingers closed, loosely spaced, then deliberately held very wide apart. It soon becomes clear that the loosely spaced option generates most propulsion.

Hold on the water

Some swimmers naturally have a very good 'feel' for the water: they find it easy to get hold of, to feel the pressure of the water against their palm. Most aren't so lucky – but fortunately, feel is something you can work on.

1. Swim freestyle exactly as normal, but with your hands closed into fists. Vary how you do this: one hand as a fist, both, three strokes with closed fists, two open, etc.

2. Notice the difference in sensation between a closed fist pushing (pretty ineffectively) against the water and your open hand.

3. Also pay attention to the feeling in your forearm when you have a closed fist. You'll notice that you can feel the pressure of water against it. This shows how it's not only your hand that provides propulsion – it's also your forearm.

Top tip

POINT YOUR FINGERTIPS DOWN!

Your pull is most powerful when your fingertips are pointing straight down, and your hand is at 90° to the bottom of the pool. Get your hand into this position as soon as possible, and stay in it for as long as possible.

▲ This swimmer has started to angle her hand down even before it has entered the water

EXIT AND RECOVERY

The exit and recovery stage should be done as smoothly as possible. It is led by the elbow, not the hand: the elbow lifts out of the water, and the forearm swings forward below it, like a broken windscreen wiper. Keep your arms relaxed and let your hand swing through quite close to the surface of the water.

The three most common mistakes people make with the recovery phase are:

- Leading the recovery with their hand, rather than the elbow
- Throwing their arm violently forward, and often out to the side as well
- Lifting their arm high in the air

▲ A relaxed-arm, elbow-led recovery

Fingertip drag and zipper drills

These drills will help you develop a smooth, elbow-led recovery phase. The zipper version is trickier: if it's a bit tough, put it aside and come back to it later when your stroke's improved.

1. Swim normally, using the high-elbow style you've developed after reading the first bit of this chapter. Once you're in a rhythm, stop lifting your hands completely clear of the water. Instead, drag your fingertips along the surface.

2. Breathe normally, and focus on maintaining a good body roll with each stroke. Keep your elbows high, so that your fingertips trace a line quite close to the side of your body.

3. You can develop this drill by having completely loose wrists and letting the back of your hand drag along the surface.

4. Try a variation known as the zipper drill. As your arm recovers, pretend you're undoing a zipper that runs from your hips to your armpit. Your thumb should never lose contact with your side.

PUTTING IT ALL TOGETHER

Having worked your way through the earlier part of this chapter, you deserve a bit of a rest. Not yet, though! There's one more drill to learn, which allows you to practise the whole arm stroke, concentrating on every aspect of it, before you start swimming using your redesigned arm stroke.

High-elbow drills

Try these drills without swim fins, but if you find your hips are dragging put some on to keep your body position streamlined.

What you need
- Possibly swim fins

1. Push off into a streamlined position. Instead of swimming alternate right-arm left-arm pull with one arm only. Make sure your focus stays strongly on keeping your elbow high for the catch, and don't allow your hand to pull in under your body.

2. Allow your body to roll down into the stroke as usual, but make sure you return to a flat, streamlined position after each arm stroke.

3. Having swum a few lengths of this, first on one arm, then the other, try the same action but with alternate strokes. This variation works best with fins: return to a streamlined position after each arm stroke, kick three or five times, then take an arm stroke on the opposite side. Don't forget to keep your head position looking down at the bottom of the pool.

◀ In this sequence, you can see clearly how the swimmer's body rolls to the side with each arm stroke, whether he is breathing or not. His hips also roll, but to a lesser degree. The image at the bottom of page 72 gives a real feeling of how the swimmer has pulled himself forward through the water. In the middle image on page 73 notice how, without a balancing arm stroke of the left arm, the swimmer's head has sunk too low.

Keys to success

- Place each hand in the water, in line with your shoulder

- During the catch phase of your pull, keep your elbow high

- Accelerate your hand throughout the pull phase

- Lead the recovery phase with your elbow, not your hand

05
BREATHING

breathe *verb* repeatedly and alternately take in and blow out air in order to function; develop flavour through exposure to air, respire, take in air, gasp, pant, wheeze

BREATHING

Lots of people have difficulty with breathing while swimming freestyle. The root cause is usually problems elsewhere in their stroke: if you get your body position, arm stroke and leg kick right, breathing fits naturally into the rhythm of your swimming. Even so, it's important to stay aware not only of how you breathe, but also why.

WHAT YOU'RE AIMING FOR

The key to breathing technique in freestyle is that it should be part of the general movement of your stroke. Unless you manage this, every time you take a breath it throws your whole technique out of balance, which causes drag and slows you down.

- Aim for a smooth turn of the head; really no more than a slight addition to the roll of your body as you take a stroke.
- Keep your neck at the same angle as usual: you're aiming to turn your head to the side slightly, not to lift it from the water.

- Make sure you have breathed out underwater *before* lifting your mouth clear of the surface. This gives you the opportunity to take on the maximum possible amount of oxygen.

▲ Taking a breath

▲ The same body and head angle, but no breath being taken

Top tip

One of the mistakes people make most often is lifting their face too far out of the water when they breathe. Remember:

ALWAYS LEAVE ONE GOGGLE IN THE WATER

If both goggles come out of the water when you turn to breathe, you've turned your head too far or are holding it at too high an angle.

BREATHING IS IMPORTANT!

It's worth recapping why we breathe while swimming. Taking oxygen on board is what allows your muscles to keep working over time. Without it, they quickly build up lactic acid, which causes a burning sensation and forces you to stop within a couple of minutes.

The only swimmers who sometimes don't breathe are 50m sprinters, whose event is over so fast that they don't have time to build up lactic acid. Anyone swimming further has to take on oxygen. For events such as triathlon, it's extremely important that lactic acid doesn't build up during the swim leg and affect you later in the race. Breathing correctly is therefore key.

BREATHE IN, BREATHE OUT

Of course, there are two elements to breathing: taking in oxygen, and expelling waste gases.

- Take all in-breaths smoothly: don't gasp or snatch at your breath, just take a smooth, deep lungful of air.
- Breathe out when your face is underwater, a steady release of bubbles that starts as soon as your face goes underwater. That way when you have a chance to take oxygen on board, you get the maximum possible amount.

BREATHING PATTERNS

Your breathing pattern is the number of strokes you do before taking a breath. Most people find it easier to breathe on one side than the other, and end up breathing every two strokes. Overall it's better to breathe every three strokes, but there are advantages to each pattern.

Breathing every two strokes.
Advantage: You get more breaths per length, making it easier to swim longer distances without building up lactic acid in your muscles.

Disadvantage: It's easy for your stroke to become lopsided and unbalanced.

Breathing every three strokes

Advantage: Your stroke has to be balanced and flexible, because you have to learn to roll your body both left and right.

Disadvantage: You can't take in as much oxygen, so sustaining this breathing pattern takes a greater degree of aerobic fitness and training.

The acid test is probably whether you just get too tired when using a three-stroke breathing pattern. If so, it may be best to use a two-stroke pattern until your fitness reaches the necessary level. Even then it's a good idea to change the side on which you breathe every length or so, so that you learn to breathe properly on both sides of your body.

HEAD POSITION

As well as affecting your body position (see page 40 for more on this), your head position has an important role to play in your breathing. Too high or low will not only cause drag but also make breathing awkward.

The ideal head position comes from your neck being in line with your spine, when viewed from the side. Look very slightly ahead, but at the bottom of the pool rather than directly forwards.

See for yourself: head position

Well, not quite for yourself: you need a friend to assess your head position. Ask your friend to pay attention to the shape of the water pushed up by your head as you swim toward them:

- If the water hits your forehead or hairline, and there's always a bow wave lifting up at the front and curving around the side of your head, your head position is too high. You need to drop your chin a bit.
- If only the back of your head is visible, and the water level never comes lower than your hairline, your head position is probably about right.
- If your head never comes out of the water at all, your head may be too low, and you need to look a little more ahead.

Kick–breathe drill

This is a really simple drill, which helps you get used to the small movement you should be making to take a breath.

What you need

- Swim fins

1. Push off and begin to kick in a streamlined position, with both arms in front of you. Take one arm stroke, but without the recovery. Instead, leave your hand straight back, next to your hip.

2. Reach forward with your leading arm, dropping the shoulder and rolling to add length. As you do this, the shoulder of your trailing arm will lift up, leaving you swimming on your side. Your head will be mostly underwater, and your neck in line with your spine.

3. To breathe, simply turn your head sideways, then lower it again. Make sure you rotate your head – don't lift it.

4. Give a few more kicks, and repeat the breath. Do a whole length breathing on this same side, then change sides for the following length.

Rolling breath drill

This drill's key aim is to establish the timing of when to take a breath. You also develop a sensation of what it's like to breathe on both sides of your body (if you don't already do so). Finally, the drill helps you to swim with a balanced stroke, returning to a streamlined position after each breath.

What you need
- Swim fins

1. Put on fins. Push off into a streamlined position, and take an arm stroke without the recovery, as on page 81. Reach forward and let your body turn into the breathing position described in step 2 on page 81.

2. Take a breath, and keep swimming on your side for a count of three. You'll find that a fast leg kick makes this drill easier to complete.

3. At the count of three, take an arm pull with your extended arm and recover with your trailing arm. Coordinate the two movements. As you roll to the other side during the arm stroke, leave the pulling arm trailing and the recovery arm extended, so that you're in the breathing position again, but facing the other side.

4. Take a breath, swim on your side for a count of three, and continue down the length of the pool in the same way.

Try to keep your movements smooth – it's tempting to snatch at the arm pull. You'll find that a strong leg kick helps, as it allows you to concentrate on the motion of your upper body.

Extra focus points
Some swimmers find the rolling breath drill tricky at first. It's worth persevering, because this drill is a great way to build up a nice, even side-to-side roll in your stroke. Once you have mastered the basic drill, bring in extra focus points:

1. Make sure that while you're swimming on your side your ear is cushioned on your shoulder. This should bring your vision perpendicular to the line of the water's surface.

2. When you take a pull and change sides, keep your vision (and head) at this angle. So, your line of vision should traverse smoothly from an on-its-side view of the edge of the pool, through looking straight down at the bottom of the pool, to an on-its-side view of the opposite wall.

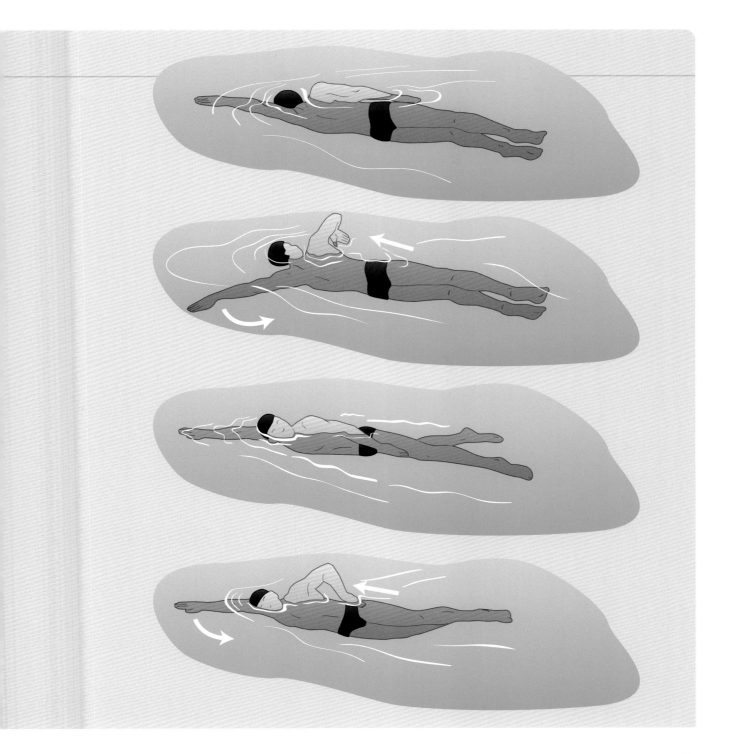

Two-pull drill

This drill adds a new element to the previous one. Now you'll be combining a breathing stroke with a non-breathing stroke. Initially, you swim breathing every two strokes, alternating sides after each length. The progression version introduces breathing on both sides during the same length.

What you need
- Swim fins

1. Put on your fins, and push off into a stream-lined position. Use a powerful leg kick: this drill works best if you're getting consistent drive from your legs.

2. Take a stroke with your left arm, but without the recovery. Leave your left arm trailing at your hip, and reach forward with your right arm. Your left shoulder will lift so that you're swimming partially on your side.

3. Swim like this for a couple of beats, until you feel settled in that position, then take a stroke with your right arm and recover your left arm. Notice the timing of when your recovery begins versus when your arm pull begins. As you do this, roll to the right, so that now your right shoulder is up and you're looking to the right side.

4. Smoothly turn your head to take a long, smooth breath, then let it sink back into the water. Again, keep the position until you settle, then take an arm stroke with your left arm, returning to the position in 2. Don't take a breath: just settle, and repeat the sequence all the way down the length.

Progression version

This drill is done with more pace. You still need a strong leg kick, but the stroke rate (the speed at which your arms move) is also higher.

▲ No breath on the left

1. Push off into a streamlined position, using a strong leg kick. Take an arm stroke without the recovery, rolling your body to the side but not taking a breath. Hold this position for a count of 2.

2. Take an arm pull with your leading arm and recover your trailing arm, rolling your body so that you're facing the other side. Don't forget to blow out a steady trail of air underwater. Hold this position for a count of two.

3. Take a third arm pull, rolling back to the side you started on, returning to the position you were in at the end of step 1. This time, take a breath as in the drill on the opposite page.

4. Repeat this breath-every-three strokes pattern, with a count of two on each side, all the way down the pool.

▲ No breath on the right

▲ Breath on the left

3–5–7 training

If you can train yourself to do it, breathing every three arm strokes is the best technique for most swimmers. It's hard work at first, and you'll probably need to increase your capacity for aerobic swimming. This exercise is really more a way of achieving this than a technique drill, but it will help you to maintain a three-stroke breathing pattern.

What you need

- Fins are useful at first: discard them as you get more comfortable with the drill

1. Swim in three-length units. Give yourself a rest of 10 seconds between each length. Swim the first length breathing every three strokes, the second breathing every five strokes, and the third every seven strokes. You don't need to be going full tilt, but don't dawdle along either: this is meant to be a lung buster.

2. Give yourself a 30-second rest, then repeat.

3. Over a period of weeks and months, make things harder, aiming to increase the difficulty whenever you feel you've got this one nailed. First, lose the fins. Next, drop the rest between lengths. Then swim in six-length units (3–5–7, 3–5–7) without a rest between them.

Keys to success

- Time your breath to fit in with the roll of your body

- Remember to keep a streamlined head position

- Turn your head to breathe – don't lift it

- Only turn as far as you need for a breath – keep one goggle in the water at all times

06
KICKING

kick *verb* propel, impel, strike out with the foot or feet

noun foot movement; leg movement, a thrashing movement with the leg or a swimming kick

KICKING

Untrained swimmers almost always have a poor leg kick. This isn't all that surprising. We tend to think that it's just using the same muscles as we use for walking around. In fact, a freestyle leg kick requires a very specific technique, strength and fitness. Get this right, and many of the other pieces of your stroke quickly fall into place.

WHAT YOU'RE AIMING FOR

The leg kick for freestyle is called a flutter kick. You kick from the hips (never the knees, though the knees do bend), causing your feet to flutter on relaxed ankles at the end of fairly straight legs. You give a strong kick at the end of your arm recovery, on the opposite side. (This happens automatically and is not something you need to do consiously.)

A good leg kick is a bit like the egg in a cake mix: leave it out, and the rest of the ingredients won't stick together. The key functions of freestyle leg kick are:

- Aiding a good, flat body position in the water
- Balancing your arm stroke
- Adding propulsion, or forward drive, to your stroke – the kick's least important job, as it provides less than a tenth of your propulsion

The flutter kick isn't a big, splashy kick. One of the most common mistakes people make is to do a large, deliberate kick from the knee, bending it almost as if they're kicking a football. Kicking like this causes drag, affects your body position and upsets your arm technique. It's like pulling a sea anchor along behind you.

KICKING RHYTHM

In freestyle, kicking rhythm is counted over a cycle of two arm strokes (one stroke by each arm). This means kicking once every arm stroke gives you a two-beat kick, twice equals a four-beat kick and three times gives a six-beat kick. Each rhythm has advantages, depending on the kind of swimming you do and your ability level.

Six-beat kick

This rhythm provides a good level of propulsion and balances the rest of the stroke extremely well. It can, though, be very tiring at first, which makes it most suited to competitive swimmers with a good, efficient technique.

Four-beat kick

This is a good basic rhythm. It provides a combination of balancing your stroke, conserving energy and providing a bit of forward power.

Two-beat kick

This provides little or no propulsion, but uses very little energy. The two-beat kick is used mainly by distance swimmers, who place a premium on endurance.

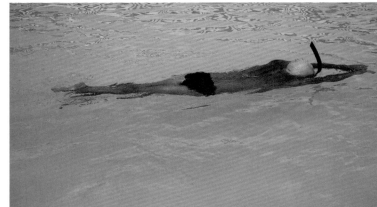

▲ The turbulence of a two-beat kick

▲ The turbulence of a four-beat kick

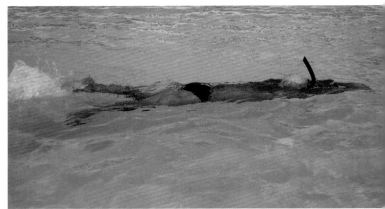

▲ The turbulence of a six-beat kick

KICK TRAINING PRINCIPLES

There are a few principles that are worth sticking to when doing technique training for the flutter kick.

1 Try not to swim head-up

Even in most swimming clubs you'll see swimmers doing freestyle kick training with their arms resting on a float and their head sticking up in the air. You don't swim freestyle with your head up in the air – if possible, don't train your body to kick in this unnatural position.

Of course, swimming with your face in the water does make breathing tricky. The best way round the problem is to use a special swimming snorkel, which instead of going to the side of your head rises in front of your nose and forehead.

▲ Using a swimming snorkel in public does require a certain degree of self-confidence, as it makes you look like an extra from a sci-fi movie. There are significant benefits though.

▲ With a swimming snorkel you can concentrate on keeping a nice, flat body position, rather than lifting your head to breathe every few seconds.

2 Use fins sparingly

Swim fins are a good training aid: they are useful in supporting your body during arm drills, and in fitness work they load your legs and build strength. Unfortunately, fins are also the crack cocaine of the swimming world: highly addictive. Nothing beats the feeling of bombing down the pool like a turbocharged human/seal hybrid. Watch out you don't get hooked. Overusing fins gives your body a false idea of what can be expected from your legs. Then, once you take them off, your technique falls apart.

▲ Fins are a useful training aid – just don't overuse them or your stroke will start to feel strange when you take them off.

Top tip

KICK WATER – NOT AIR!

It can be tempting to make a big splash with your kick: it *feels* like you must be generating lots of speed. But you're swimming in water, not air.

Any time your feet come out of the water, they're waving at the spectators rather than driving you forward.

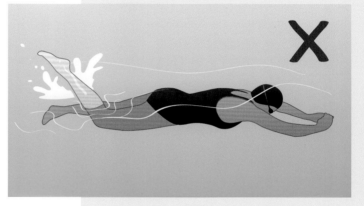

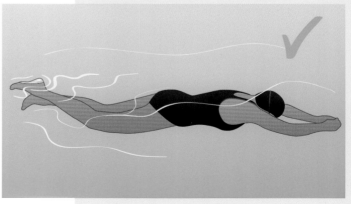

Kicking: setting the flutter kick

Doing this drill several times allows you to set the muscle memory for how a flutter kick should feel. It's also useful if you feel your kick has gone off-track in some way: just haul out on the side of the pool and run through the exercise.

What you need

- A clear poolside with a raised edge (this drill is harder in pools where the deck is the same height as the water surface)

1. Sit on the edge of the pool, with your bottom on the deck and your thighs clear of it. Lean back and rest your weight on your hands, then extend your legs out straight over the water.

2. Point your toes, and keep your legs close together. Lower your feet until they're about 30 cm underwater. Make sure your toes are still pointed.

3. Keeping your legs straight, lift one foot steadily up, but don't let it break the surface. Lower it again, raising the other foot in an opposite movement. Your feet should be close together as they pass.

4. Steadily increase the speed of the movement, relaxing your ankles so that they flutter up and down as you kick. As you get faster, aim to make the water boil without making any splash at all.

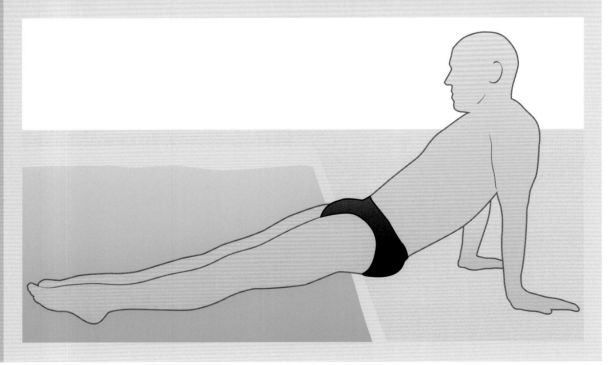

Flutter kick practice

One of the problems coaches often see is swimmers who use a big leg kick. This causes all kinds of problems, including increased drag and poor body position. Fortunately, practising a proper flutter kick usually brings quick results. This drill is not about getting to the end of the pool as fast as possible. It's about practising the range of movement.

What you need
- Kickboard
- Possibly a swimming snorkel

1. Hold the kickboard by its side, as shown in the photo, with just your thumbs over the top and your fingers underneath. You're aiming to swim with relaxed wrists and bent elbows dangling down, rather than holding the kickboard out in front of you with straight arms.

2. Push off and start kicking. Look down at the bottom of the pool. Use the limited range of movement from the drill on page 94, opposite: keep your legs straight, your toes pointed, and kick from the hips. Your knees should be stiff, but not rigid.

3. You'll feel a rocking movement in your hips; try to keep your head still and your upper body still and relaxed. Breathe out steadily as soon as your face is underwater, which will help you to relax.

4. If you're not using a swimming snorkel, lift your head to breathe when necessary, but keep kicking. Notice how lifting your head affects the angle of your hips and legs, and forces you to start bending your knees as you kick.

If you feel your leg kick getting clunky and big during a swim, a few lengths of this drill will remind your body of what it should be doing.

Kicking: building power

Many swimmers fail to get what they need from their leg kick because they only kick down, with the top of their foot and their shin. This drill encourages you to develop the other stroke of your leg kick: the upstroke, using the bottom of your foot and your calf.

What you need
- A small area of pool where you're out of your depth

There are three versions of this drill, each one increasingly difficult. When you can manage the third, hardest version it will be a good sign that your kick is really effective.

Version 1 – least tough
Float vertically in water that's well out of your depth. Cross your arms over your chest, palms flat. Kick hard to keep your head above water, using the flutter kick described at the start of this chapter.

Take care not to start using an eggbeater kick, a kind of alternate breaststroke kick used by water polo players to lift their torsos out of the water.

Ideally, try to maintain the exercise for at least 30 seconds before stopping for a 15-second rest, then repeating it. Doing this a total of five or six times each session should be enough.

Version 2 – harder

In this version of the drill, instead of crossing your arms over your chest you lift your hands free of the water. Just keep your hands and forearms in the air, with your elbows below the surface.

Version 3 – very testing

This time, instead of putting only your hands in the air, lift up both arms into the streamlined position shown on page 43. You'll have to kick very hard even to get your head above water for a breath. Only try this version when you're comfortably able to complete five or six repetitions of the second iteration of this drill. Otherwise you risk swallowing a magnum of pool water and putting yourself off swimming forever.

Kicking: building strength

This is a land-based training technique you can do anywhere. It builds leg strength, improves technique and strengthens your core.

What you need:
- A comfortable place to lie down
- Ideally a fellow swimmer

1. Lie on your back, with your hands tucked under your bottom, lifting your hips slightly.

2. Raise your legs straight off the ground by about 20 cm, and flutter your feet, flicking your ankles as fast as you can. Do this without consciously bending your knees: try to make the movement come from the hips and thighs.

3. Keep this up – with your feet fluttering as fast as you can possibly manage – for 30 seconds. This is when having someone else there for encouragement helps!

4. Lower your legs and have a rest for one minute. Repeat at least once.

As you get better at this drill, build up the time from 30 seconds to a minute and increase the number of repetitions you do.

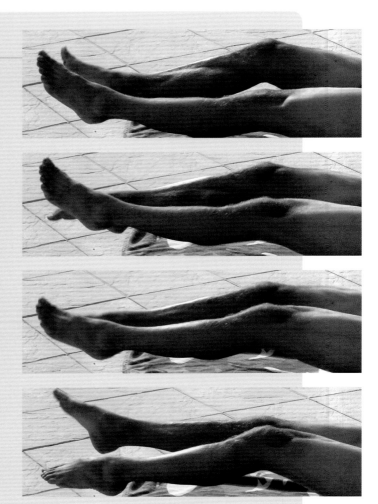

Top tip

FLEX YOUR ANKLES

Ankle flexibility is a crucial part of the flutter kick. Improve yours by sitting with your ankle over your knee, gripping your heel and toes, and winding your foot in circles first one way, then the other, for a minute in each direction before changing feet.

Kicking: building strength

This is an advanced land-based drill, which helps improve both leg strength for kicking and core body strength. It requires good balance and a certain amount of flexibility. Take this drill steady, and if your back or neck (or both) feel painful or uncomfortable, ease yourself back to a lying-down position and stop.

What you need
- A yoga mat or similar cushioning

1. Lie flat on your back with your arms by your sides. Bend forward, and with a slight rocking-back motion get your hips in the air, supported on your hands. Your elbows should be below your hips, resting on the floor. Your legs will be in the air, knees bent. Your weight rests on your hips and shoulders.

2. Straighten your legs so that they point up in the air. Gently lower your right leg forward and your left leg slightly backward. The two movements should balance each other out, allowing you to stay comfortably upright.

3. Bring both legs back to vertical, then perform the same movement in reverse. Take care to move slowly, to keep your hips solidly planted on your hands, and not to extend your legs too far and topple over. Repeat the movement five times on each side, alternating sides, then gently let yourself roll back to a sitting position.

Keys to success

- Use small flutter kicks, not big splashy ones

- Kick from the hips, not the knees

- Kick without breaking the surface of the water with your toes

- Keep your ankles loose and relaxed

07
STROKE
AND RHYTHM

rhythm *noun* pace, tempo, cadence, pulse, a regularly recurring pattern of activity, or repeated functions of the body

STROKE AND RHYTHM

In this last key section, the focus is on fitting everything together: combining good body position, arm stroke, breathing and leg kick into a smooth, easy, efficient style. This is where you're aiming to become one of those swimmers who just glides smoothly along: a stylist, rather than a splasher.

WHAT YOU'RE AIMING FOR

Aim to swim freestyle with a feeling of moving continuously and smoothly forward. If your stroke feels lurching, as though there are kinks or dead spots slowing you down, try to analyse where these are coming from and go back to the relevant sections of this book.

To recap the basic elements of a good freestyle swimming technique:

- Keep your body straight and flat in the water
- Swim with your neck in line with your spine, looking at the bottom of the pool rather than the wall
- Put each hand into the water in line with your shoulder, and begin the pull with a high elbow. Avoid pulling in underneath your body
- Move arm and hand through the catch, in-sweep and out-sweep phases with increasing speed
- Kick your legs in a continuous flutter kick, kicking from the hips without consciously bending your knees

Head position, breathing

At first, most swimmers find this drill something between very tricky and impossible because they're used to swimming with their head held too high. It does come to you pretty quickly, though, and it's a really good drill to return to again and again. It reminds you of good head position, body roll and breathing technique.

What you need:
- A small, not-too-squishy ball, a bit bigger than a tennis ball

1. Tuck the ball between your chin and your chest.

2. Push off, and start swimming. Try to keep the ball in place, not only as you swim along but also when you breathe.

3. Don't tense up: remember to keep your jaw and neck relaxed. You're aiming to hold the ball in place, rather than clamping it tightly down.

Three-quarter catch-up

This simple drill is good for many elements of your stroke. It emphasises the extension and glide of the hand entry and catch phases of your stroke. The drill is also a good way to develop roll and breath timing, and done without fins it plays up the role of your leg kick in maintaining a good body position.

This drill can be hard work aerobically when done without fins, so is probably best tackled one length at a time, with a 15-second rest between lengths.

What you need
- Swimming lane with line along the bottom
- Swim fins for some versions

1. If you want to focus on arm technique and timing, put on swim fins. For all-round stroke development, leave the fins on the poolside.

2. Push off along the line, concentrating on keeping your head and the centre line of your body directly above it. Take an arm stroke, leaving the other arm extended in front of you.

3. Delay the pull of your extended arm until the recovering arm is just about to enter the water. Repeat this stroke and rhythm with the other arm, and carry on all the way down the pool.

There are several versions of the catch-up drill. Two of the most useful are full catch-up and reverse catch-up.

Full catch-up
This is essentially the same drill as three-quarter catch-up, but harder. Instead of starting your arm pull as the recovering arm is about to enter the water, wait until it has slid beneath the surface and is starting to extend.

Reverse catch-up
This drill demands (and so trains you to) a greater level of coordination between body roll and breathing. In reverse catch-up, instead of one arm being stretched out unmoving in front of you, it rests by your side with your hand by your hip. This is basically putting the 'stop' in at the other end of your arm pull, before the recovery instead of after.

▼ **Full catch-up**

Tarzan-and-Jane

This advanced drill is great for checking how well you're able to keep your body swimming straight, without twisting or kinking. It's a good one for open-water racers, including triathletes: it helps you get a sense for swimming in a straight line without being able to see where you're going the whole time.

I call this the Tarzan-and-Jane drill, because I started doing it when I was a kid, after seeing Jonny Weissmuller and Maureen O'Sullivan, as Tarzan and Jane, swimming like this in a jungle pool.

What you need
• Swimming pool with line along the bottom

1. Push off along the line, and take one stroke of front crawl. Reach ahead with your arm and let your body start to roll to the side as usual.

2. Instead of stopping the roll, let your body turn right over on to your back, with your leading arm still extended. Then take a stroke of backstroke with the other arm.

3. Continue the rolling motion in the same direction back on to your front, taking another stroke of front crawl.

4. Restart the sequence of the same three strokes – front–back–front – by taking another stroke on your front with the opposite arm.

All the way down the length, aim to keep swimming above the line on the bottom of the pool. It seems impossible at first, but it does get easier!

Fitness-training version
You can also use a version of this drill as part of your fitness training. Instead of just one stroke each, front–back–front, do two strokes on your front, then three on your back. Keep this rhythm all the way down the length, do a length of straight freestyle to recover, then repeat. Sets of 100m or 200m at a time, with a 15- or 20-second rest between each, are an aerobic challenge for any swimmer.

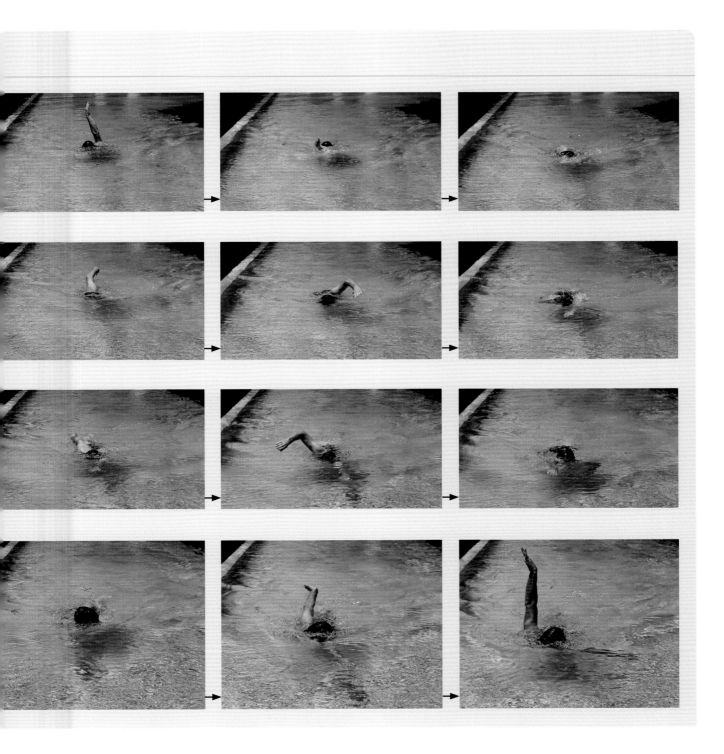

SWIM MINDFULLY

Even for good swimmers, it's easy to forget technique when you're training for fitness, or aiming at a timed event such as a triathlon. Doing this will almost always cost you in the end. You can have the highest possible degree of fitness, but if your technique causes drag, that fitness won't do you much good.

Even in the midst of training hard, put aside time for technique. You'll get more from this if you can fit in separate technique-work sessions, but few of us have unlimited time. If you're going through a period when all your pool time is needed for fitness swimming, fitting the next exercises into the start of a training session can be a useful sharpener for your stroke.

One-arm swimming

This drill is good for establishing arm rhythm and breath timing, as well as overall technique. At first you may find it easier with swim fins and/or a pull buoy, though these are really a bit of a crutch – as your leg kick improves, try to set them aside.

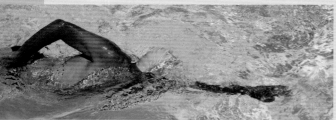

What you need:
- Possibly swim fins and a pull buoy (worn together these help you keep a nice, flat body position: the buoyancy of the fins keeps your feet up even if you don't kick)

1. Push off into a streamlined position. Start your stroke as usual, but keep one arm reaching out in front of you the whole time. Take arm strokes only with the other arm.

2. Focus on making sure you have good body roll, and breathe on your pulling-arm side. Breathe as infrequently as possible, but don't let the drill become an aerobic challenge: you need to be swimming within yourself, rather than gasping for air.

You can swim a whole length using just one arm, or take a certain number of breaths before changing sides. I prefer to change sides every four to six strokes, as it feels more balanced, but experiment to find the pattern that works best for you.

Trailing-arm variation

This harder variation of the one-arm drill works your technique in a different way. In this version you leave your non-pulling arm trailing at your side, rather than reaching out in front of you, and breathe on the non-pulling side.

The focus is on what your pulling-arm side is doing as you roll away from it to take a breath, and on timing the breath. It's easy to start waggling your body, so stay aware of the need to keep a long, flat, streamlined position.

◀ This is a tough drill, and under stress this swimmer has lifted his head, compromising his streamlined position in the water. He is, though, showing a very nice high-elbow pull.

Butterfly drill

I include this drill in almost every warm-up. It combines a freestyle arm stroke with a butterfly leg movement. The drill loosens up your torso, gives a really strong feeling for swimming on your side, and a feel for the rotation of your hips and kicking action as you breathe.

1. Push off the wall and take an arm stroke. Keep your other arm extended, and breathe on this first stroke, as you would coming to the surface after a turn.

2. After the recovery, stay rolled to the side and take a second arm stroke with the same arm. Use the forward movement of your arm as it enters the water and the turn of your head after the breath to create a butterfly motion of your body. Let this motion wave down your body, ending in a kick.

3. After two arm strokes on one side, repeat the pattern on the other side, pulling with the other arm, rolling your body in that direction and breathing on a new side.

SWIMMING BLIND

You *do* need an empty lane to try this! But it's a really good way to judge how straight and balanced your stroke is. Most of us are constantly making teeny little body adjustments to keep swimming in a straight line. These are based on visual inputs that you don't consciously register. Take them away, and a truer idea of how balanced your technique is will emerge.

I also find swimming blind is a useful way of concentrating on how your stroke feels. It's amazing how much easier it is to sense the effectiveness of your arm pull, or the degree of water resistance you're experiencing, with your eyes shut.

Start by swimming along above a line on the bottom of the pool. Initially, just close your eyes for three or four strokes before opening them to check where you are. As your feel for how to swim straight with your eyes shut improves, you'll probably be able to keep them closed for longer periods.

This exercise is excellent for open-water swimmers, who need to be able to swim straight without sighting on the bottom of a pool or by looking at lane lines. As an illustration, World Open-Water Swimmer of the Year 2009 and 2011 Keri-Anne Payne attributes part of her success to the fact that she learnt to swim without goggles, couldn't really see where she was going and had to develop a feel for swimming in a straight line.

WATCH YOURSELF

A friend of mine once told me that she'd been terribly upset at some photos of herself at a wedding. 'I don't *look* like that! That woman's shorter and rounder than me. *I* look like Lana Turner.'

The terrible truth is, of course, that we rarely look as we imagine. As a result, most people's swimming improves when they get a chance to watch themselves swim. They immediately see where their stroke differs from a really expert swimmer's.

Filming swimming

The ideal scenario is for a friend to film you swimming. This is likely to be impossible in a public pool, as they generally don't allow cameras. If you can get access to a private pool, though, it's worthwhile getting a friend with a video camera to

▼ Filming swimmers can be tricky, as people are rightly sensitive to cameras in swimming pools. If you can get permission to film, though, the benefits of seeing yourself swim are tremendous.

shoot some footage. Warm up first, and do a bit of swimming before the camera rolls, so that your stroke is working as it would in normal circumstances.

Use lights and shadows

Sometimes pools with lights in the walls can give you a glimpse of your stroke. It's a bit like trying to get a glimpse of yourself in a shop window while cycling past, but if you swim at night, the lights will probably cast a shadow that's defined enough to give you some idea of how your stroke is looking.

Keys to success

- Keep your head in a good, streamlined position, and roll your body with every arm stroke

- Swim with your eyes closed every once in a while, to assess whether your stroke is balanced

- Take opportunities to watch yourself swim, in order to spot glitches in your technique

08
TURNS

turn *verb* twist, rotate, go round, roll, twirl, move to face a different direction, move around an axis

TURNS

They're not actually part of *swimming* technique, of course, but lots of people want to learn tumble turns, because they're a good way of improving the distance you can cover in a set time. If you're aiming to do a triathlon with a pool-based swimming leg, it's also worth learning how to do faster touch turns – tumble turns aren't allowed in some triathlons.

WHAT YOU'RE AIMING FOR
The three key elements of a tumble turn are a fast tumble or flip, timing, and a strong, streamlined push off the wall.

- For a fast tumble or flip, you need to initiate the turn in a snappy way, and bend your body into as compact a shape as possible

- Timing your turn relies on a combination of your distance from the wall and the speed at which you're approaching it
- A strong, streamlined push off the wall allows you to travel further underwater in a streamlined position

OPEN-WATER TURNS
Most triathlons have an open-water swim leg, rather than a pool leg. The course is usually laid out around one or two buoys, which all the swimmers have to pass at least once to complete the distance. Most novice triathletes get badly snagged up at these turns: turn to page 145, in the open-water chapter, for advice on how to avoid that happening to you.

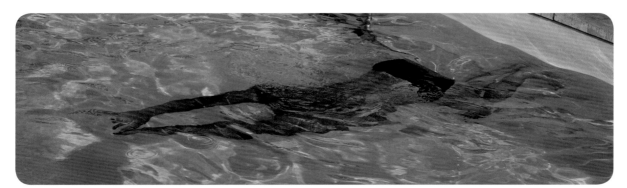

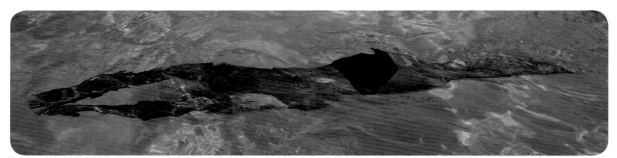

▲ A streamlined push off the wall

The push-off: strong and streamlined

1. Hold on to the side of the pool, and bring your legs up so that your feet are against the wall about 60 cm below the surface. Have one foot above the other, with your shoulders similarly canted.

2. Let go with your hands and let your body slide down under the surface. Keep your body bent into a compact shape, like a coiled spring. Turn your feet and body so that you're sideways. Make sure your feet are firmly planted against the wall.

3. Push off as hard as possible. If one or both feet skid off the wall, or one foot pushes more strongly than the other, your foot position is wrong: have another try.

4. Once you've found a good, planted foot position, take a few goes to fix it in your head. This is what you'll be aiming for after learning to tumble.

5. Now add a streamlined glide, with your hands either one on top of the other or thumbs touching and your head tucked in. At the start of the glide you'll be on your side, and by the end of it you need to have drifted round onto your front.

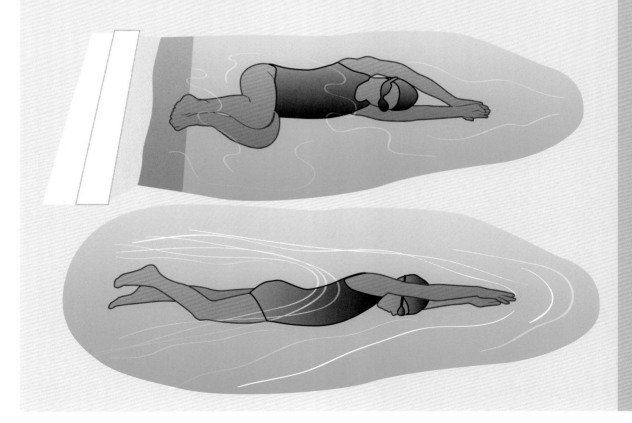

Top tip

To avoid getting a snootful of water while learning tumble turns:

MAKE SURE YOU'RE FOREVER BLOWING BUBBLES

Keep blowing a trickle of air from your nose all the way through the tumble turn, to stop water going up your nose.

Getting used to tumbling

Lots of swimmers get disoriented about which way is up when they try to learn tumble turns. They quickly get a snortful of water up their nose, come up coughing and spluttering, and give up. The trick to learning a tumble turn is to break it down into stages. This drill is the first step: getting used to tumbling underwater.

1. Push off the wall, but instead of adopting a streamlined position, push off with both hands by your sides.

2. Before you lose too much momentum, tuck your chin into your chest and start a forward-roll motion. Lead with your head, and aim for this to be a snappy and definite movement.

3. Let your body, then your legs, follow your head around. Make your body as compact as possible, so that you tumble over quickly, and bend your legs too. Only take a breath when you've come back to the surface facing the same way as you were moving.

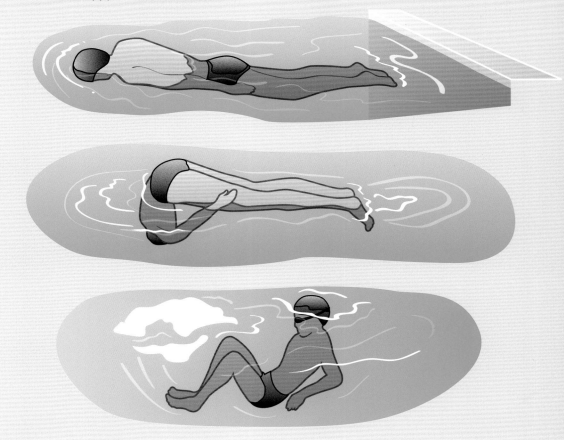

Arm stretch tumble

This drill first adds an element of stretching your arm out in front of you to tumble over, then of swimming into the tumble.

1. Push off the wall as in the drill on page 119, except with one arm extended in the streamlined position. Have the other arm against your side.

2. Before you lose momentum, perform the tumble. The movement is similar to the one shown on page 121, but this time it's your arm that drives it, rather than your head: begin an arm pull, but continue the motion underneath your body, as if reaching back toward the space between your knees.

3. Let your head follow, and then the rest of your body as on page 121. As before, keep blowing a constant stream of bubbles from your nose: only stop and take a breath when your head comes to the surface.

4. Practise this drill with both right and left arm stretching forward: later on this will mean you can turn whether it's your right or left arm that makes the last stroke of the length.

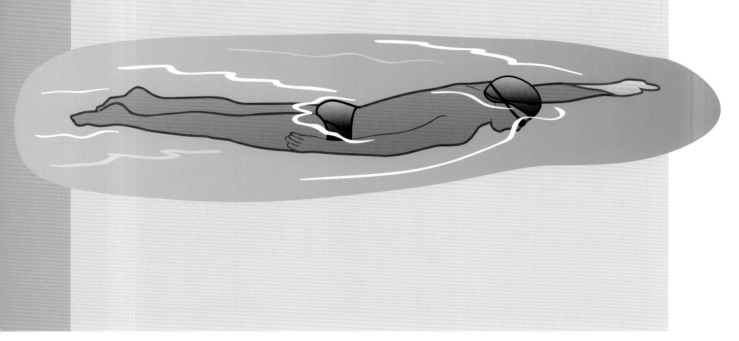

Leading with your arm

This drill simply adds together two skills you already have: swimming freestyle and tumbling. It also teaches you how the angle at which you drive the turn with your arm affects the angle at which you tumble.

1. Push off the side of the wall into the streamlined position, then start swimming. Take a breath as you come up to the surface, then two or three strokes.

2. As you finish an arm stroke, perform the tumble you learned on page 122. Practise this on each arm, left and right.

3. Now try varying the angle at which your hand initiates the tumble. Instead of reaching between your knees, see what happens if you reach outside your left knee or right knee.

Note how this affects the angle at which your legs come over during the tumble. For example, reaching outside your left knee with your right hand will mean your legs tumble over to the right-hand side, rather than directly over the centre line of your body.

Timing

The only way to learn the timing of your tumble turn – when to start the tumble in order to plant your feet solidly on the wall – is through trial and error. The variables include your degree of flexibility, the speed at which you tumble, and the pace at which you approach the wall.

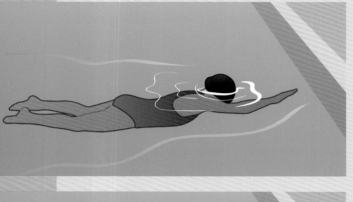

1. Swim toward the wall at the end of your lane. For the last few strokes, it's OK to look ahead more than you usually would. When you feel you're one or two strokes from the end of the lane, allow yourself to glide forward with one arm extended. Start your tumble once your hand's about 50 cm from the wall.

2. You're aiming to tumble over very slightly short of the wall, as your momentum will carry you a small way. Aim to land with your legs bent and your feet squarely on the wall. Your body should be sideways, rather than fully upside-down: apply the knowledge you got from the drill on page 123 to achieve this.

3. For now, just keep practising, adjusting the point at which you tumble until you always land with your feet solidly planted on the wall.

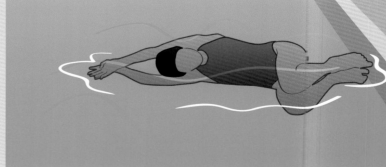

▼ Underwater kick, dolphin

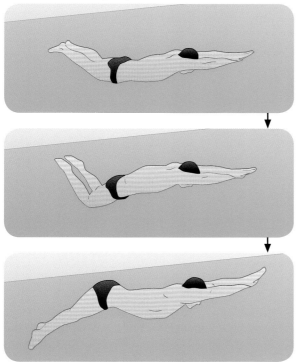

▼ Underwater kick, freestyle

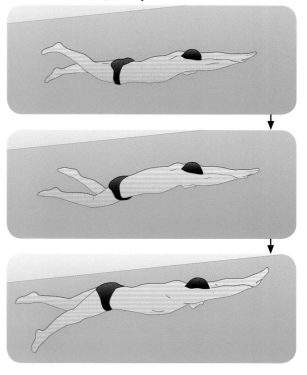

DRIVE FROM THE WALL

The final element of a good tumble turn is your drive away from the wall. Doing this well can gain you a lot of ground. It also sets you up to start swimming from a moving, rather than a standing, start. Four key elements have to be combined to get good drive.

1 Pushing off strongly

This depends on having your feet planted firmly on the wall in a position that means they won't slip. If you find this is a problem, go back to the drill on page 124 and practise more. Never push off down, toward the bottom of the pool; push off parallel to the surface, at the same depth as you ended up after the tumble.

2 Rotation back to a face-down position

After pushing off, you need to rotate your body so that instead of being on your side, you're facing the bottom of the pool. As this is achieved, step 3 will already have begun.

3 Kicking to maintain momentum

Top swimmers kick underwater to maintain speed and delay the moment when they come back to the surface. Some swimmers do this using a flutter kick, most prefer to use butterfly kicks. If you have enough breath for this, experiment to see which suits you best.

4 Surfacing strongly

Getting maximum drive from the wall requires striking a balance between distance and speed. Never let yourself slow down underwater to such an extent that you're gliding slower than you would be swimming. It's important to get back to the surface while you're still travelling at a good speed. Otherwise, your first few strokes will be spent wasting energy getting you back up to swimming speed.

TOUCH TURNS

Tumble turns are barred in some pool-based triathlons, making it a good idea for triathletes to work on fast touch turns. If you have a pool-based swim like this coming up, give up tumble turns entirely for a couple of weeks beforehand. Otherwise you're almost certain to forget yourself in the excitement of the event, throw in an accidental tumble turn and get disqualified.

Practise this technique using both left and right hand to touch the wall; that way, you won't compromise your swimming by trying always to finish on the same hand.

1 One-handed touch

You only need to touch the wall with one hand. The best way to finish is very like a tumble turn, but instead of leading the tumble with your hand you leave it extended to touch the wall. You need your hand either gripping a rail or the edge, if either is available, or flat on the wall of the pool.

2 Push back

Bringing your legs tightly in under your body, at the same time push away from the wall with your hand, dropping your opposite shoulder back, away from the wall. Your non-pushing hand stays under the surface.

3 Plant and drive

You should now be sideways (looking left if you touched with your right hand, right if you touched with your left). As your feet plant on the wall, let the pushing hand drop through the air and in front of your head. Drive away from the wall as on page 127.

 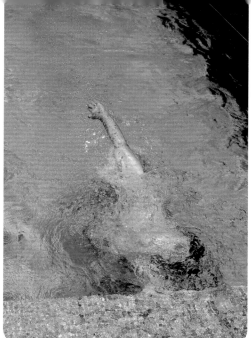 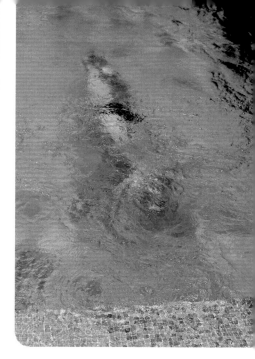

Keys to success

- Make turns snappy and sharp

- Keep blowing a stream of bubbles from your nose while tumbling

- Plant your feet so that you get a strong drive off the wall with both feet

- Don't use turns to rest. If you need a rest, stop and take one

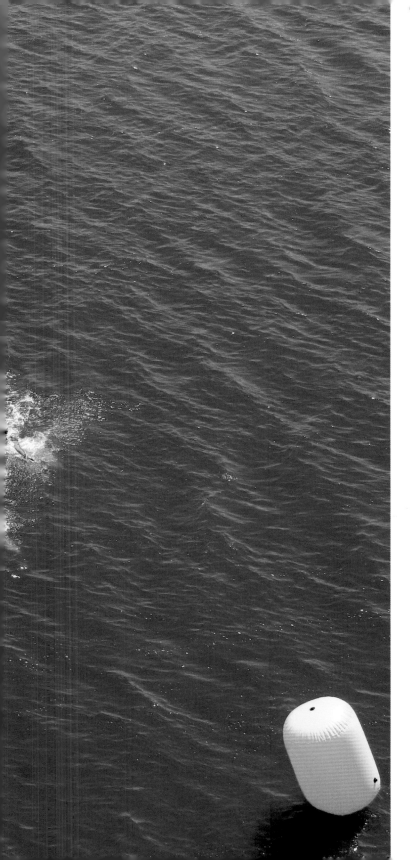

09

OPEN WATER

open water *phrasal noun* outdoor expanse of water, usually sea, river, lake, or reservoir, esp. that used for swimming

OPEN WATER

Most people get their first taste of serious open-water swimming when they take part in a triathlon or a charity swim. You may have bought this book with just that sort of swim in mind. If so, everything you've read so far will come in useful, but this chapter will add a few final hints and tips that should make the challenge even more fun.

OPEN-WATER EVENTS

Open-water swimming actually encompasses a tremendous range of types of swimming. The simplest is wild swimming – taking pleasure in swimming somewhere other that a chemically sterile pool. At the other extreme is open-water racing, long-distance endurance events in which the world's top swimmers race for hours, and usually finish just

seconds apart. There are also solo endurance swims such as Channel crossings, swim-trek holidays and even open-water orienteering.

Whatever kind of open-water swim you're planning, they all have a few things in common. Adaptability and a willingness to swim without lane lines or guides are key.

- You'll need to be able to adapt your stroke to the water conditions and temperature.
- You'll need to prepare for different swimming environments (i.e. how many other swimmers are in the water with you, and where the swim is taking place).
- It's important to adapt your training so that it suits the kind of swim you're planning to do.

SWIM WITH A TRAINING PARTNER

As with any sport, your training needs to mirror the thing you're training for. If you're taking part in an open-water event, this obviously means some, at

least, of your training should be done in open water. It's a really good idea to do this with a training partner. Ideally you want another swimmer of about the same standard as you, but you could also go out with a kayaker, SUP paddler, paddleboarder, etc.

There are two key benefits to a training partner:

Safety: Open water, particularly the ocean, is potentially a lot more dangerous than pool swimming. Having someone with you makes things a little safer.

Motivation: The open-water environment can be a bit off-putting on cold, wet days. Knowing someone else is relying on you to come out helps. Having someone swimming alongside also helps you to push your level, rather than sitting back and taking it easy.

Of course, you'll also get to share the joy of lake sunrises on misty mornings, swimming into a warm beach at sunset, and so on.

OPEN-WATER EQUIPMENT

The basics of open-water equipment are the same as for pool swimming: goggles, swimming costume, hat and earplugs. Some contests – Olympic open-water races, for example – have strict rules about the type of costume you can wear. In these, the only extra equipment you're likely to need is petroleum jelly, to stop chafing and prevent other swimmers grabbing hold of your shoulders or feet.

Some competitions, such as triathlon swims in water below a certain temperature, insist on you wearing a wetsuit. You can buy these relatively inexpensively, and it's worth doing so if you plan on swimming in open water a lot. The alternative is to rent one for the event, but this is expensive, you can't get used to the wetsuit beforehand, and there's no guarantee the fit will be good.

PICKING A WETSUIT

Never be tempted to swim in a wetsuit that's not specifically designed for swimming. It won't have articulated shoulders, and fighting the fabric with every arm recovery will drain your arms and shoulders of energy very quickly.

A quick Google search will tell you which companies make swimming wetsuits: among the main brands are 2XU, Aqua Sphere, Ironman, Orca and Speedo, but there are lots of others. Decide on your price point, and try on as many as you can. It's really worth visiting a shop: there's no substitute for seeing how the suit actually fits your body shape. It needs to be as tight as possible but not constrictively short or draggily long.

Getting out of your wetsuit

In a triathlon, you have plenty of time to get into your wetsuit, but you'll want to get out of it as fast as possible in order to start the bike leg. The only way to get good at this is to practise, at the end of open-water training sessions.

1. As soon as you emerge from the water, start running toward your bike. Reach behind and grab the puller ribbon on your wetsuit.

2. With the other hand, undo the Velcro tab that holds most wetsuits closed. Next pull down the zipper.

3. Peel off first one arm, then the other. Then peel the suit down to your waist. The wetsuit will be half inside-out at this point.

4. When you reach your bike, bend over and peel down/step out of the wetsuit legs.

TECHNIQUE: ARM STROKE

The arm stroke for open-water front crawl is essentially the same as for pool swimming. As in the pool, a smoother, more efficient stroke uses less energy for the same speed. This is probably even more important in open water: events are over longer distances, so the effect of tiny inefficiencies is magnified.

One difference from the pool is in stroke rate: open-water swimmers generally swim with a higher arm cadence than pool swimmers, of between 73 and 85 strokes per minute.

ADAPTING TO CONDITIONS

Open water swimming sometimes – nearly always, in fact – forces you to adapt your technique to the conditions. The key change is that if the water is choppy, a higher recovery of the forearm and hand is needed. This avoids your hand or arm being caught in the chop or wave face.

You may also have to adapt your breathing pattern: if waves are coming from the left, breathe to the right, and vice versa. That way you're less likely to swallow what feels like a small bucketful of water with each stroke.

Body-rotation mixed drill

Good body rotation is as important in open-water swimming as it is in the pool. This mixed drill is hard work when done without fins, so it's best to start with them on until you're comfortable with the drill.

What you need
- Swim fins
- Pull buoy

1. Push off in a streamlined position, but with your arms by your sides instead of stretched out ahead. Kick with a steady rhythm.

2. Keep looking downwards, not forwards. Take breaths on alternate sides, simply by rolling your body. Don't move your arms or turn your neck to breathe, just roll your body.

3. After one length, take off your fins and put your pull buoy between your ankles (not your thighs as usual) or calves. Swim two lengths like this, concentrating on rolling your body with each stroke.

4. Take a 10- or 15-second rest, and repeat until you have done 15 lengths in total.

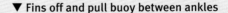
▼ Fins off and pull buoy between ankles

Top tip

USE YOUR KICK FOR BALANCE, NOT SPEED

In open-water events, which tend to be over longer distances, your kick's key job is to maintain your body position and balance your arm stroke, *not* to provide forward movement.

Aim to make small, neat kicks. If your feet sometimes cross, pointing your toes will help prevent this.

TECHNIQUE: LEG KICK

The leg kick for open-water is the same as for pool swimming, a flutter kick. There's no need to make big changes, though a kick with low amplitude (the distance your feet move from top to bottom) creates less drag.

KICKING RHYTHM

If you normally use a four- or six-beat kick, you may want to adjust your kicking rhythm. Kicking your legs isn't a very energy-efficient way to get propulsion, and over the long distances of open-water events a high kicking cadence is very draining. If you're about to climb on to a bike and ride 40km, then run 10km, this is a particularly bad idea.

As a result, endurance swimmers and triathletes rely less on their legs than pool swimmers, except at the start or finish. They mostly use a two-beat kick, and gain less than 5 per cent of their propulsion from their legs. As a comparison, pool swimmers get closer to 10 per cent of their propulsion from their legs.

Head position, direction, and sighting

The most streamlined head position for freestyle is to be looking straight down, rather than ahead. In the pool, most swimmers are forced to compromise this: they need to avoid crashing into people in front, and to spot the wall for turns. These aren't problems in open water, so it's possible to keep a perfect head position most of the time.

The only difficulty is that in an open-water swim you need to check where you're going from time to time. Training to swim in a straight line is a big help, and the exercise on the opposite page should be useful. But you will still need to 'sight' – lift your head to see whether you're on course for the turn or finish you're aiming for:

1. Finish breathing out until your leading hand enters the water.

2. Lift your head forward while pressing down (rather than pulling back) with your leading hand. At the same time, kick harder.

3. As your head rises, take a mental photo of the course, and immediately drop it back down into the streamlined position. Don't take a breath – if your head comes out that high, you've lifted it too far.

4. Take an arm stroke, during which your body rolls to the side allowing you to take a breath as usual.

Balanced-arms drill

This exercise is useful for a) finding out whether one of your arm strokes is more powerful than the other, and b) correcting imbalances. In open water, balanced arms will make it easier to swim in a straight line.

You will need
- Fins
- Pull buoy

1. Push off in a streamlined position, with fins on and the pull buoy between your thighs.

2. Swim a timed 50m using only your right arm. Concentrate on maintaining a high elbow during the pulling phase, and breathe every three or four strokes.

3. Repeat with your left arm, then run through the whole exercise twice more (so you'll have done 3 × 50m on each arm).

4. Average out your times on each arm. If one is significantly slower, work on improving that arm's stroke.

Some coaches recommend wearing a hand paddle to strengthen a weak arm. A better alternative is probably to use volume training: do one-arm drills in units of three, with two on your weaker arm and one on the stronger one.

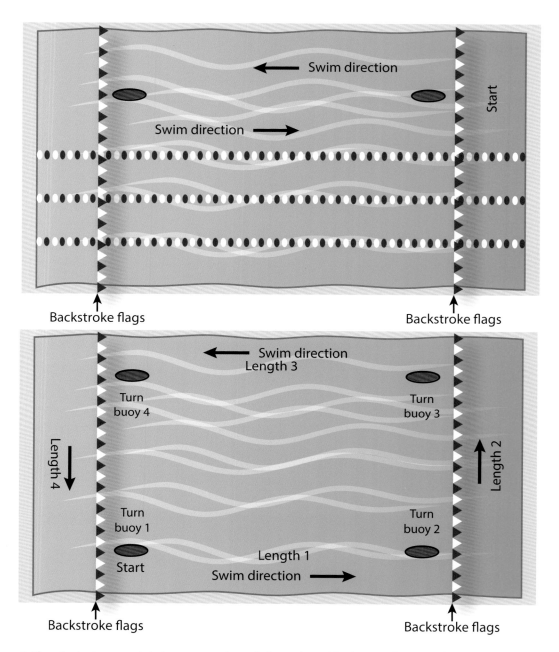

Swim direction

Swim direction

Start

Backstroke flags

Backstroke flags

Swim direction
Length 3

Turn buoy 4

Turn buoy 3

Length 4

Length 2

Turn buoy 1

Turn buoy 2

Start

Length 1
Swim direction

Backstroke flags

Backstroke flags

▲ If you're lucky enough to have access to a whole pool, positioning turn buoys at the corners, near the backstroke flags, gives you a big area of water to work with. You can swim along the edges, between the corners in an X shape, in a Z pattern ... wherever you imagination (or your coach) leads you. Even if some of the pool is taken up with other swimmers and you can only get a couple of lanes, a pair of turn buoys allows you similar training options.

TRAINING FOR OPEN WATER

The key difference between pool and open-water swimming is the lack of turns. In a 25-metre pool you rarely actually swim more than 20m at a time. Then you get a push off the wall, which gives you a chance to break the swim. In an open-water event, you may swim a kilometre or more without interrupting your rhythm. If you don't practise for it, this comes as quite a shock.

Pool training

It sounds obvious, but before you enter a 1km or 1.5km open water swim, you need to make sure you can swim that distance continuously. (In fact, it's a good idea to build up to 130 per cent of your event distance.) This can be done in a pool, though ideally not in a single lane, as you need space to turn around without touching the wall and this can be cramped in a single lane's width.

The ideal is to get access to a whole pool, though a couple of lanes is enough. If you set up buoys in opposite corners, you can swim the entire race distance without touching the sides or breaking your stroke.

Training with other open-water swimmers in the pool also gives you the chance to swim in conditions you'll experience in the event. Try all setting off together, for example, to get a feel for swimming in crowded water at the start. Follow other swimmers, or swim beside them, to get a feel for drafting.

Paceline training

One good exercise for anyone planning an open-water swim is to train in a paceline. You need at least three swimmers, and no more than five. The paceline allows everyone to build endurance, even in a mixed-ability group. It works in pretty much the same way as on a bike:

1. Set off in a line, with each swimmer close behind the one in front. You need to be almost touching their feet.

2. After a set distance or time, the leader pulls off the front. In a pool, it's best just to stop after, say, 100m and let everyone else go by; in open water, the leader can just drift back after a minute on the front, then tag on to the back of the line. (If you've got a kayaker or someone who can blow a whistle at one-minute intervals, it makes this a lot easier.)

3. The new leader swims the same distance, before rotating back and allowing the swimmer behind to come through.

All the swimmers need to have similar abilities, but you can make adjustments to fit quite a wide range. If stronger swimmers take longer pulls on the front, and weaker swimmers either take shorter turns or miss them, a fairly mixed group can train together.

Top tip

ONCE IN A WHILE, DO A FARTLEK SESSION IN THE POOL

Fartlek is really a run-training style, which is designed to improve both aerobic and anaerobic performance. The basic idea is that you're continuously moving, but varying your pace.

In a pool, you can do this by swimming between the backstroke flags, rather than to the end of the pool, then turning without touching the bottom or sides. Vary your pace: a few full-out sprints, some relaxed swimming and some race-pace all jumbled together.

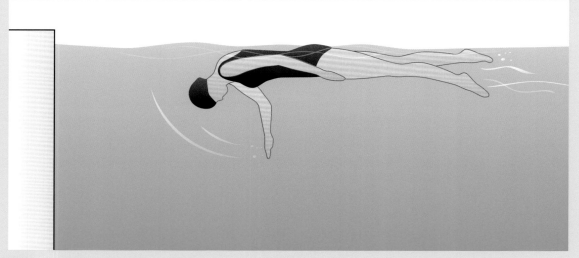

▲ This swimmer is doing a tumble turn short of the edge of the pool, so that she won't be able to push off. Starting to swim from a motionless beginning places much greater demands on your fitness and technique than an ordinary turn. Putting a few short turns like this into your training is a good way to vary your sessions.

Open-water acclimatisation

Although you can train for an open-water swim in the pool, try to include at least a few open-water swims in the lead-up to your event. Not only that, also try to make sure the open water you train in is similar to event conditions. For example, there are fewer benefits to training in a river or lake if your event's going to be in the ocean. Key things to bear in mind include:

1 Water temperature: Some open-water events do not allow wetsuits, even though they take place in relatively cold water. The Channel swim is one example, but there are plenty of other, shorter ones. Cold water is particularly tricky to get used to, and the process can take months of acclimatisation. At the start, you may only be able to manage a minute in the water. The only consolation is that your body does adapt, and it does get easier.

Warmer water than you're used to also poses problems, but adaptation is less painful! You can mimic the effects of warm water by pool swimming in a wetsuit.

2 Water conditions: The open-water racing at the 2007 World Aquatics Championships in Melbourne was an event for the tough nuts, among the tough world of open-water racing. The competitors had to swim through large blooms of jellyfish, and some of the favourites failed even to finish. It's an extreme example, but it does show that open-water swimmers need to be ready to face unexpected challenges, including waves, boat exhaust fumes, seaweed, fog and tidal currents.

OPEN-WATER SWIMS

If you've never done an open-water swim event before, it can be a bit daunting. Before the event, consider where to position yourself and how to get the most from your swim. This depends to some extent on your aims. If you want to compete at the front, you'll be mixing it with a bunch of ambitious, sharp-elbowed swimmers. If you want simply to enjoy the swim and finish feeling you've done well, a more relaxed approach will work better.

Starts

Swims often begin with a massed start. The racers will try to position themselves wherever they have the shortest route to the first turn buoy. When the starter's hooter goes, this area will be a churning maelstrom of arms and legs, as people sprint to get clear water and a good position. If you'd prefer a more leisurely start, either move off to the side or let the competitive swimmers get going for a few seconds, then swim behind them.

Turns

Turns offer competitive swimmers a golden opportunity to take time out of other racers. Turning as close as possible to the buoy, without losing speed, can gain you several metres. Of course, that means the area close to the turn buoy becomes a pinch point: if you're not competing, and want only to enjoy your swim, you may think it's a better idea to give the buoy a wider berth.

Rounding a buoy

This is a good exercise for competitive open-water swimmers. It gets you corkscrewing round a turn buoy very quickly.

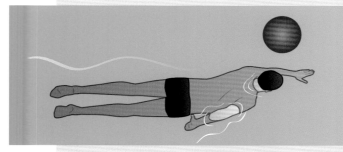

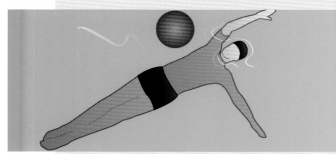

You will need
* Ideally, an anchored buoy

1. Swim at the buoy, sighting a couple of times as you get close to it.

2. Aim to swim very slightly past the buoy, taking a stroke with the arm closest to the buoy (your left) as you come past.

3. Instead of taking another front crawl stroke, continue the roll of your body so that you turn on to your back. As you do this, twist slightly toward the buoy.

4. Take a stroke of backstroke with your other arm. Use this to continue to roll in the same direction, taking you back on to your front.

With practice, this will get you round a 90° turn very fast, without the need to lift your head, do a little bit of breaststroke, etc.

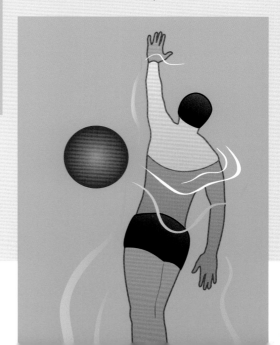

SWIM STRATEGY FOR TRIATHLON

If you are swimming open water as part of a triathlon, it's worth thinking about how your swim will fit with your overall performance. Bear in mind that triathlons are never won on the swim leg. To get a good overall performance you'll need to balance two key elements: finishing position versus energy expended.

Unless you're a very strong swimmer, pushing yourself to keep up with a fast group will leave you too tired for the bike and run legs. In general, it's better to finish the swim feeling somewhat within yourself, rather than as if you're about to throw up through the effort. (Save that sensation for the run.)

Practising in open water will give you a clear idea of your maximum sustainable pace. Try to fix the rhythm of your stroke in your head. It's possible to buy aids to help with this, including head attachments that tap out a preset rhythm, and watches that count the number of strokes you take each length.

Navigation practice

Navigation is a combination of efficient sighting and swimming straight toward a buoy or finish. Swimming straight for 25m, then efficiently sighting, will make any open-water swim easier. It does take practice, though!

You will need
- A small cone
- A coach or helper

1. Position your coach or helper, armed with the cone, at the opposite end of the pool. (This exercise requires a pool that's pretty much empty, or it can be done 20m or so out from the bank of a river, lake, etc.)

2. Push off the wall and start swimming. While you are underwater, your assistant will be putting the cone down somewhere along the far edge of the pool.

3. As you come to the surface, take a stroke or two and then sight as on page 138, looking for the cone.

4. Swim to the cone without sighting again, aiming to finish your length as close to it as possible.

OPEN-WATER SWIMS

If you get really into open-water swimming, there are some fantastic events around the world that make a great excuse for a trip away.

Bosphorus Cross-Continental: follow in the flipperprints of Lord Byron, in this annual swim down the Bosphorus from Asia to Europe.

Damme-Brugge Open Water: a 5km race along a Belgian canal, which was first held in 1910.

Hyde Park Christmas Morning Swim: every Christmas Day, a bunch of loonies turns up to swim in the Serpentine, in London. It's only 90m from one side to the other, but it's very, very cold.

Manhattan Island Marathon Swim: one for the serious distance swimmers, 46km around Manhattan Island in New York.

Swim Around the Rock: 5.2km around Alcatraz Island in San Francisco Bay, where swimmers must contend with icy water, strong currents and the possibility of being eaten by sharks.

Swim Thru Perth: 2.2km and 4km swims in Perth, Australia, to Matilda Bay. This swim is famous for having competitors ranging from 10 to 80+ years of age.

Waikiki Roughwater Swim: a 3.9km swim across Waikiki Beach in Honolulu, Hawaii. This swim is said to have inspired the swim leg of the first-ever Ironman race.

Keys to success

- Keep your stroke smooth

- Maintain a streamlined head and body position

- Adapt breathing patterns and arm recovery to the conditions

- Prepare by swimming in open water, as well as the pool

TECHNIQUE TRAINING SESSIONS

If you want your swimming to improve, you really have to work constantly on your technique. This is particularly true if you've introduced a new element to your stroke – the high-elbow pulling action, for example. If you've been swimming in a particular style for years, it will take a long time for a new style to become automatic. Until then, you'll need to keep reminding yourself at regular intervals.

WHEN TO WORK ON TECHNIQUE

You're not likely to achieve much if you only ever work on your technique *after* a hard training session, when you're tired. It's easy to slip into thinking you should be training hard, getting fitter, getting stronger, but none of these will bring you as much benefit as improving your technique. It's best to devote a whole swim purely to technique work: your body and mind are fresh, and you concentrate harder, getting maximum benefit from your time in the water.

Alternatively, if your time in the pool is severely squeezed, you could make technique work part of your warm-up, or spend the first part of the session doing drills, before getting into the fitness part of the session.

SPEED VERSUS QUALITY

Whenever you're doing any of the exercises or drills in this book (or any others that you've developed for yourself), try to make an active decision *not* to go fast. There's an old saying that applies here: 'First, do it. Then, do it right. Last, do it fast.' Technique work falls into the second category: do it right. If you try to add speed, it will detract from your ability to control your movements with precision.

Top tip

For most people, it's worthwhile getting an experienced coach to provide an analysis of your style, and give you key areas for improvement. Try to limit these to three key elements, for example:

1 KEEP YOUR HEAD ANGLE LOWER, BY LOOKING AT THE BOTTOM OF THE POOL RATHER THAN AHEAD

2 PLACE YOUR HAND IN THE WATER IN FRONT OF YOUR SHOULDER

3 STOP BENDING YOUR KNEES WHEN YOU KICK

Think about the three key improvements *whenever* you swim, rather than only when you are specifically working on your technique.

Session 1

Duration

- 20–30 minutes

This session focuses on improving the side-to-side roll of your body as you take each stroke. Concentrate on smooth transitions from one side to the other.

Warm up

Swim 400m, broken down into:

- 50m front crawl
- 50m butterfly drill (see page 112)
- 50m front crawl
- 50m backstroke, concentrating on rolling your body with each arm stroke
- 50m front crawl
- 50m breaststroke
- 100m front crawl

Set 1

- 4 × 50m, with a 15-second gap between each 50m

Do the kick–breathe drill on page 81. Focus on keeping your ear cushioned on your shoulder, and make sure you're seeing the deck of the pool as a vertical line (i.e. your head is flat in the water, rather than tilting up).

- 2 × 50m, 15-second gap

Swim full stroke at a steady pace, rolling your body into a similar position as the one you were just using during the drill.

Set 2

- 4 × 50m, with a 20-second gap between each 50m

Move to the progression version of the first drill, which is shown on page 85. Because you're breathing every three strokes, this may be more tiring: if 20 seconds rest isn't enough, take longer.

Use your vision to assess the angle and movement of your head. Your sight should sweep *across* the direction in which you're swimming. Imagine a line perpendicular to your line of travel, crossing it at the point where your eyes look straight down at the bottom of the pool. If your vision follows this line, your head is turning from side to side without lifting.

Warm down

It's a good idea to throw in something different for a warm-down:

- 4 × 25m kick, as shown on page 95
- 4 × 25m alternating Tarzan-and-Jane (page 108) with full stroke

Session 2

Duration
- 20–30 minutes

This session focuses on two elements of front crawl style: improving your breathing and making your leg kick more efficient.

Warm up
Swim 400m, broken down into:

- 100m front crawl
- 6 × 50m alternating leg kick with fins and a float, then arms-only with a pull buoy (leave the fins on for extra floatation)
- 100m front crawl

Set 1
- Sinking practice

Warn the lifeguards you're about to do this, or they might think you're drowning and jump in to save you.

Tread water in the deep end, then take a deep breath and allow yourself to float vertical in the water. Immediately begin to breathe out in a controlled, steady way. Keep breathing out until you start to sink (it may take longer than you expect). You're aiming to sink to the bottom and sit there cross-legged.

- 8 × 25m, 15-second gap between each 25m

Follow the drill on page 95. Each time you take a breath and your face goes back in the water, begin to breathe out steadily as in the sinking practice above. Only lift your head when you need to take a breath.

(Notice how lifting your head to breathe affects the angle and action of your leg kick: your legs sink lower, and you start to bend your knees more, both of which cause drag.)

Set 2
- 8 × 25m

Move to full-stroke three-quarter catch-up (or full catch-up if you prefer) as on pages 106–107. As above, breathe out constantly and steadily; rather than taking a breath every two or three strokes, breathe only when you need to.

Warm down
- 4 × 100m butterfly drill (see page 112), backstroke, breaststroke, front crawl, all done lazily

Session 3

Duration
- 30 minutes plus

This session focuses on developing an effective leg kick, one that balances your stroke and contributes to a good body position in the water, but without creating drag. Ideally, the first set would be done with a swimming snorkel, if you have one and they're allowed in your local pool.

Warm up
Swim 400m, broken down into:

- 100m front crawl
- 200m alternating front crawl and back-stroke every 25m
- 100m front crawl

Set 1
- 8 × 25m, 15-second gap between each 25m

Follow the drill on page 95. Whether or not you have a swimming snorkel on, remember to keep breathing out a steady stream of air. This stops your upper body from being too buoyant, and helps you to relax your torso and keep it still. Your movement should be from the hips, with stiff knees and loose ankles.

Set 2
- 4 × (3 × 25m), 20-second gap between each 75m

This set is in parcels of three lengths. Swim the first length following the drill on page 95 but without a swimming snorkel. Hold a pull buoy on top of your kickboard (this is just to get it down to the other end of the pool, so you only have to do it on this first length of the set). For the second length, put your float on the side of the pool and put the pull buoy between your legs, then swim back arms-only (some people like to put the buoy between their calves, rather than their thighs). For the final length, put the pull buoy on the side of the pool and swim full stroke.

As you swim the third length, try to pull together the sensations from the previous two lengths: first, a neat, steady flutter kick; second, a sensation of your legs being close to the surface and supported.

Warm down
- 4 × 25m kicking backstroke, holding the sides of a float above your head
- 50m fingertip-drag drill (page 71)
- 50m steady front crawl

Session 4

Duration
- 20–30 minutes

This session is a good way of reminding yourself of the angle your head should be at – which is one of the biggest problems for many swimmers who want to improve their stroke.

Warm up
Swim 400m, broken down into:

- 100m front crawl
- 100m single-arm pull, alternating arms on each length as on page 110
- 100m kicking, as on page 95
- 100m front crawl

Set 1
- Body position float

Warn the lifeguards you are doing this, or they may think you have fainted in the water. The aim is to fix in your mind a flat, streamlined position in the water, which you'll carry through into the main set:

- 8 × 25m kick, 15-second gap between each 25m

Follow the drill shown in steps 1 and 2 on page 135; using fins makes this drill easier, as it creates more of a bow wave for you to breathe behind. Focus on keeping your body as flat and straight in the water as possible and on looking directly down as you swim along.

As your upper goggle breaks the surface, make sure the line of the surface splits your vision perpendicularly. This tells you that your head is not lifting forward as you breathe.

Set 2
- 8 × 25m, 15-second gap between each 25m

Do the rolling breath drill on page 85. Focus entirely on the angle of your head as you breathe, trying to keep one goggle in the water and making sure the line of the water's surface splits your vision, as above.

Warm down
- 200m, alternating 50m front crawl full stroke, 25m Tarzan-and-Jane (pages 108–109), 25m catch-up (pages 106–107)

Session 5

Duration
- 20–30 minutes

This session focuses on the high-elbow action; this is tricky to learn if you have previously swum in another style, so it's worth revisiting regularly.

Warm up
Swim 400m, broken down into:

- 100m front crawl
- 200m alternating front crawl and backstroke every 25m
- 100m front crawl

Set 1
- Lane-line initiation

As a reminder of the sensation you're looking for, do the lane-line practice described on page 64 a few times.

- 8 × 25m pulling drill, 15-second gap between each 25m

Follow the drill on page 72. Focus on putting your hand into the water in front of your elbow, making sure it does not drift inward,* then beginning your pull with the same motion as you practised on the lane line.

*Notice the way your body rolls as your arm takes a pull, and returns to a flat position as your hand re-enters the water. This return to a flat position can cause your hand/arm to drift inward. Stopping this from happening needs a conscious effort.

Set 2
- 8 × 25m three-quarter catch-up

Move to full-stroke three-quarter catch-up as on pages 106–107. Breathe only when you need to, rather than following a set pattern. Concentrate on keeping the same high-elbow position as in the single-arm drill above.

Warm down
- 4 × 25m kicking backstroke, holding the sides of a float above your head
- 50m fingertip-drag drill (page 71)
- 50m steady front crawl

Session 6

Duration
- 20–30 minutes

This is more a fitness session for open-water swimmers than a technique session, but it allows you to practise sighting and technique for turning around a buoy.

Warm up
Swim 400m, broken down into:

- 50m front crawl
- 50m butterfly drill (see page 112)
- 50m front crawl

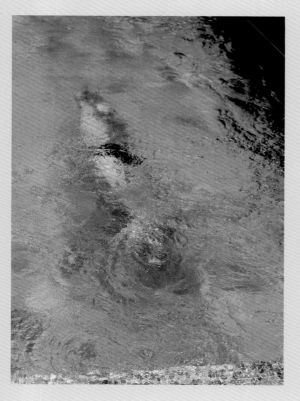

- 50m backstroke, concentrating on rolling your body with each arm stroke
- 50m front crawl
- 50m breaststroke
- 100m front crawl

Set 1
- 5 × 200m, 30-second gap between each 200m

This set should be swum at race pace: not exhausting, but enough to raise your heart rate toward the top of your aerobic threshold.

Each 200m is swum without touching the end of the pool to turn. Instead, perform the open-water turn shown on page 145. If there's a pace clock at the end of the pool, use the sighting technique shown on page 138 to check your speed at 100m. If not, place a towel or float at the end of the lane and use it as a target to sight on.

Set 2
- 400m front crawl

The point of this set is mainly to vary your pace. Swim the first 50m at race pace, then drop to an all-day speed for the next 25m. Next throw in 25m of slightly brisker swimming, and then another 25m of flat-out sprinting. Drop down to race pace for 50m, then do 25m at all-day pace. Repeat, but without stopping.

Warm down
- 4 × 100m, each 100m made up of 25m butterfly drill (see page 112), backstroke, breaststroke, front crawl, all done lazily

ABOUT THE AUTHOR

Paul Mason is a former international swimmer, British champion and record holder. Today he combines a career as a writer with coaching swimmers and running the successful Swim Better Fast technique clinics. He is also a keen surfer, cyclist and snowboarder.

Paul's talents as a swimmer first became evident – though probably only to his Dad – when he placed 16th in the national age-group championships at the tender age of 11. A couple of years of hard training later, he won his first international race at a Home Nations competition in Scotland.

At 13 Paul broke into the national junior team after winning a silver medal at the national championships, and he went on to race internationally for two seasons. He also captured the national short-course 100m and 200m records. Paul then retired from swimming, in search of a girlfriend who didn't always smell of chlorine.

In his mid-twenties Paul found his way back into swimming, racing at masters level and working with other swimmers to help them to improve their technique. Gradually he began to realise the lack of help available for older swimmers who wanted to get better, and were fit enough to do so, but were being held back by their technique.

All Paul's coaching is based on a simple principle: drag is your enemy. The *Swim Better, Swim Faster* approach has proved extremely popular with triathletes and keen leisure swimmers alike, as these happy former students will tell you:

'It's like a new beginning. I felt before that I needed to get fitter and stronger to improve my swimming. Now I know the truth.'

'It all now seems less complicated than I've been making it.'

'I normally dread our swimming sessions, but this showed us how to use our training to better effect, rather than just slogging up and down the pool.'

'I improved my open-water swim time by 12 per cent.'

'One of the poolside lifeguards has just told me how well I'm swimming compared to when he'd last seen me. I gave you full credit for my improvement!'

INDEX

3–5–7 training 86
alcohol 37
ankle bands 19
ankle flexibility 99
arm stretch tumble drills 122
arm strokes 57–73
    bent-arms scull 63
    the catch 61, 64
    drag, reducing 58–59
    exits 70
    fingertip drag 71
    hand entry 59–60
    hand shapes 67
    high-elbow drills 72–73
    high-elbow scull 65
    in-sweep 66
    lane line initiation 64
    out-sweep 66
    recovery 70
    straight-arms scull 62
    underwater action 61
    zipper drills 71

balanced-arms drills 139
basic swimming technique 14–19
bent-arms scull 63
body position 17, 39–55
    body rolls 48–51
    head position 40–41
    hip position 42
    shoulder position 42
    streamlined position 43–47
body rolls 48–51
body-rotation mixed drills 135
breathing 16, 75–87
    3–5–7 training 86
    kick–breathe drills 81
    patterns 78–79

progression drills 85
rolling breath drills 82–83
two-pull drills 84
butterfly drills 112

carbohydrate intake 37
costumes 18

diet 37
drag 43, 47
    reducing 58
drills
    arm stretch tumble 122
    balanced-arms 139
    body-rotation mixed 135
    butterfly 112
    full catch-up 106–107
    high-elbow 72–73
    kick–breathe 81
    reverse catch-up 106–107
    rolling breath 82–83
    two-pull 84
    zipper 71

earplugs, benefits of 18
eating 37
efficiency, front crawl 16
equipment 18–19
    open-water swimming 132
events, open-water swimming 148

fartlek training 142
filming, benefits of 114–115
fingertip drag 71
flexibility 21–37
    ankles 98
flutter kick 90, 94, 95
focus 10

food 37
front crawl arm pull 14–15
full catch-up drills 106–107

goggles, benefits of 18, 113

hand entry 59–60
hand shapes 67
head position 40–41, 43
    breathing 105
    open-water swimming 138
high-elbow drills 72–73
high-elbow scull 65
hip position 42

improvement, pace of 10
in-sweep 66

kickboards 18, 95
kick–breathe drills 81
kicking 17, 89–101
    ankle flexibility 98
    flutter kick 94, 95
    power, building 96–97
    rhythm 90–91, 136
    strength, building 98, 100
    training principles 92–93

lane line initiation 64

mindfulness 110

one-arm swimming 110–111
    trailing-arm variation 111
open-water swimming 10, 129–149
    acclimatisation 143
    adapting to conditions 134
    balanced-arms drills 139
    body-rotation mixed drills 135
    equipment 132
    events 148
    fartlek training 142

head position 138
kicking rhythm 136
navigation practice 147
paceline training 141
rounding a buoy 145
starts 144
techniques 134, 136
training for 140–142
triathlon strategy 146
turns 118, 144
wetsuits 132–133
out-sweep 66

paceline training 141
Payne, Keri-Anne 113
pool training 140–141
pull buoys 18
pushing off 119

reverse catch-up drills 106–107
rhythm and stroke 103–115
    butterfly drills 112
    head position, breathing 105
    kicking (open water) 136
    one-arm swimming 110–111
    swimming blind 113
    Tarzan-and-Jane 108–109
    three-quarter catch-up 106–107
rolling breath drills 82–3

Scaravelli yoga 23
sculls
    bent-arms 63
    high-elbow 65
    straight-arms 62
shoulder position 42
snorkels, use of 18–19
straight-arms scull 62
streamlined position 43–47
stretching techniques 22–23
    crossed-forearms stretch 30
    hip stretches 28

leg stretches 32–33
reaching-behind stretch 31
shoulder stretches 30–31
side stretches 29
sun salutation 24–27
stroke and rhythm 103–115
butterfly drills 112
head position, breathing 105
kicking (open water) 136
one-arm swimming 110–111
swimming blind 113
Tarzan-and-Jane 108–109
three-quarter catch-up 106–107
swim fins 18, 93
swimming blind 113
swimming costumes 18
swimming for weight loss 37

Tarzan-and-Jane 108–109
techniques
basic swimming 14–19
breathing 16
stretching 22–33
timing turns 124
touch turns 126

training partners, benefits of 130–131
triathlon strategy 146
tumbling 121–122
arm-stretch tumble 122
turns 117–127
drive from wall 125
leading with arm 123
open-water 118, 144
pushing off 119
timing 124
touch turns 126
tumbling 121–122
twisting 52–54
two-pull drills 84

warming up and down 23, 34–36
legs 34–35
shoulders 35
upper body 35
weight loss, swimming for 37
wetsuits 132–133

yoga, benefits of 23

zipper drills 71